THE SOYBEAN FAMILY TREE
Tasty, Thrifty, Vegan Food
by BOBBI PARKER

Drawings by Bobbi Parker

Just Be Publications
Paradise, California

THE SOYBEAN FAMILY TREE
Tasty Thrifty Vegan Food
by Bobbi Parker

Drawings by Bobbi Parker

Other books by Bobbi Parker
Johnbe and the Bobkins

Printing, May 1998

JUST BE PUBLICATIONS
5785 Fickett Lane - Paradise, CA 95969
(530) 877-3570

Printed in the United States of America
With Soy Ink and 10% Post Consumer and 50% Recycled Paper

Publisher's Cataloging-in-Publications
(*Provided by Quality Books, Inc.*)

Parker, Bobbi.
    The soybean family tree : tasty thrifty vegan food / by
Bobbi Parker.
    p. cm.
    Includes index.
    ISBN 0-9663878-0-5

    1. Cookery (Soybeans) 2. Soyfoods. 3. Vegan cookery.
I. Title.

TX803.S6P37 1998   641.6'5655
                          QBI98-497

DEDICATION

This book is lovingly dedicated to my daughter Susie, who finally decided she wanted to learn how to cook. Her request that I do a vegan workshop for her, and some of her friends, is the spark that caused this book to be written. Her considerable computer skills have made a valuable contribution as well.

TABLE OF CONTENTS

PREFACE

While I wrote this book to share my everyday recipes, I found that there is a flood of new scientific evidence coming forward at this time, linking the use of soy products to improved health in areas such as cancer prevention, lower cholesterol, easier menopause and increased bone density in post menopausal women.

Probably the best known and most respected medical researcher in this field is <u>Dr. Andrew Weil the founder of the Center for Integrative Medicine in Tuscon, Arizona.</u> As I read his books, I found that they reinforced many of my own beliefs and attitudes with sound research. I was even more impressed by the fact that he restored his own health by integrating the things he learned into his personal life.

While his program addresses many aspects of health, one recurring theme is the value of soy based foods. I have selected excerpts from one of his best selling books "8 Weeks to Optimum Health", that reinforces that idea. (Used by permission). Pgs 68 through 71.

"...I want you to learn about the wonders of soybeans...

"Besides being cheaper, soybeans are better than animal foods in several ways. Their protein does not come with a load of saturated fat that will stimulate your liver to make cholesterol. They also contain isoflavones, unusual compounds that may offer significant protection against cancer...researchers also call them phytoestrogens, meaning plant-derived estrogen like substances.

"Some ailments, breast cancer in particular, are increasing at alarming rates throughout the world. One theory explains the rise in terms of increased exposure to foreign estrogens, not those made by a woman's own ovaries.

"It is well known that estrogenic hormones are used as growth promoters in animals raised commercially for food; residues of these hormones find their way into beef, pork, poultry and dairy products...

"You can only do so much to prevent these toxins from entering your body, but phytoestrogens in soybeans offer a sound defensive strategy.

"Japanese women have much less trouble (than Americans) with menopausal symptoms, probably because they get protective phytoestrogens in their diet. And there is reason to think that these compounds afford men protection from prostate cancer...

"...whenever possible, try to buy soy products made from organically grown soybeans."

INTRODUCTION

This all started when I got excited about the surprising amount of delicious, healthful and inexpensive vegan food one can prepare, based on a pound of soybeans which cost less than a dollar. I found out that one pound of soybeans makes _seven quarts of Soy Milk or fourteen ounces of Tofu,_ and leaves behind _five cups of Okara (soy pulp),_ that has many tasty, nutritious uses.

My enthusiasm seemed to be contagious. People started expressing an interest in having me organize a workshop. Originally, my purpose in creating this booklet was to put in writing the recipes I might want to use, so people could take them home. I visualized taking a morning and demonstrating the making of soy milk, tofu and okara.

It seemed like a good idea to make some dishes from these freshly made foods and serve them for lunch, right there on the spot. It sounded simple enough. You see it all of the time on TV.

Actually I knew better. As a professional Artisan, I knew that the road between the conception of an idea and completion of a marketable product has always been a slippery slope.

The obvious first step was to write down the recipes that I intended to demonstrate so they could be taken home for future use. When I really got started, the ideas flooded in and this little booklet just grew and grew until it became a book. I'm seriously considering making a cooking video. From the beginning, I had the concept of the soybeans being like a tree trunk with three basic branches, soy milk, tofu and okara. Next I saw recipes branching off and dividing again and again until it looked like a tree. It is my hope that people will take my recipes as a starting point and grow their own branches of _The Soybean Family Tree._

PART ONE - QUALIFICATIONS, PHILOSOPHY AND BASIC TERMS

I'm writing this book for those who want to adopt a vegan lifestyle, but have no idea where to begin. Old habits die hard and it is important to develop some new ones. I hope to give you some answers to the old questions, "What's for dinner" or "What do I take to the picnic?" Most of us find a few recipes we like and repeat them until we're tired of them. Then we switch to something else and forget our former favorites. I have provided a place in the back of the book for you to list some of your new favorite dishes or combinations and when you draw a blank, read them. If you are a beginner turn to "Tips for New Cooks" on page 64.

I have prepared a list of all of the ingredients used in the recipes to help you keep your cupboard stocked. Quick and easy meals are only easy if you're prepared in advance. In order to take it out of the cupboard or freezer, it has to be in there in the first place. The whole concept of THE SOYBEAN FAMILY TREE is to spend a few hours in the kitchen preparing ingredients or complete dishes for many meals.

Chapter One
QUALIFICATIONS AND PHILOSOPHY

What are my qualifications? I'm neither a dietitian nor a chef. I am an old-fashioned good cook with fifty years of experience. I like my food to be delicious and easily prepared. Necessity has also dictated that it be inexpensive. When I decided to adopt a vegan diet, instead of focusing on what I had given up, I chose to take a good look at what I had to work with, and to see how many interesting foods I could prepare. I've always been inventive in everything I do and cooking is no exception. As a result I found that I could start out with some soy beans and after a morning in the kitchen I could end up with enough fresh food for many meals, and ingredients or precooked foods, for many more.

I want to make it clear that I am in no way an expert. The few times I expound at all on nutrition, I'm just stating my own opinion or quoting my choice of experts. There are hundreds of schools of thought about nutrition, and anything you can name has some experts lined up for and some against. Even if two of them are for the same things, they may not be for having them at the same time, or cooking them in the same way.

I have no need to convert anyone to my way of eating. I personally choose to be at least ninety five percent vegan, and I reserve the right to decide when to make those few exceptions, without guilt or explanation. I offer this material to you freely, in that same spirit.

There are many good vegan recipes and products I've never tried. This book is my way of sharing a specific group of recipes that I've developed to use in my everyday life.

This book has recipes for anyone who wants good meatless, dairyless meals, whether they are full-time or part-time vegans. Their reasons may be political, spiritual, or health concerns such as allergies or high cholesterol. It's economically sound, too.

≪≫ ≪≫ ≪≫
Chapter Two
BASIC TERMS

I'm one of those old-fashioned cooks who seldom measure anything. I've attempted to be specific where I need to be and still offer a variety of personal choices. I want to give you some general information about the terms I've used in these recipes that may keep you from asking, "What does she mean by that?"

All of the recipes in this book are part soy milk, tofu or okara (soy fiber), and they don't call for any animal products. There are optional ingredients listed, however, all recipes may be prepared without them. They are generally no-fat or-low fat, and use minimal amounts of sugar. I believe that it is preferable to use organic foods and filtered water whenever possible. This is especially important in the making of soy milk.

UTENSILS

These recipes were all designed to be prepared in an ordinary kitchen with ordinary utensils. My personal favorites for the stove top are IRON SKILLETS or STAINLESS STEEL SAUCEPANS and KETTLES that are aluminum clad on the bottom for more even heating.

For baking I use GLASS or POTTERY BAKING DISHES and METAL COOKIE SHEETS.

The term NON-STICK in my recipes means I use either NON-STICK SPRAY or NON-STICK PANS.

I DO CHOOSE TO USE A MICROWAVE. I was very surprised at how often I used it. One obvious use is for thawing ingredients from the freezer such as soy milk and okara, or finished products like stuffed buns or lasagna. It's also very handy for starting long cooking ingredients while you prepare the rest of the ingredients in the recipe. I recommend glass or pottery containers, rather than plastic for long cooking in the microwave.

A food processor is nice, but not necessary. I've mostly used a MINI FOOD CHOPPER, a BLENDER and a HAND BLENDER.

A GOOD GARLIC PRESS is an important investment. My favorite one is so easy and convenient to use, it has greatly increased my use of fresh garlic. It takes whole cloves of garlic, skin and all, and in an instant produces a maximum of fresh pureed garlic, without waste or mess. A small tool, that makes cleaning a cinch, is attached. To my surprise, this garlic press works equally well on fresh ginger or chopped onions!

A COFFEE GRINDER is a very valuable tool, even if it never sees a coffee bean. Coffee grinders are very inexpensive and readily available. They are good for making soy coffee (see page 61), and for grinding many whole seeds, herbs and spices, most of which retain their flavor and nutrition longer in storage if left whole. Spices just taste better, and things such as flax seeds deliver more of their beneficial nutritional value, when freshly ground.

OILS AND FATS

It is generally agreed that a diet low in fat is desirable. Just how much fat and what kind is controversial. Eliminating animal products from your diet is a big step in reducing cholesterol-producing fat, as well as reducing total fat grams.

THERE IS NATURAL OIL IN SOYBEANS, thus in soy milk, tofu and okara, however, it is unsaturated, and without cholesterol. When

I use the term NO-AT I mean no additional fat.

The term LOW-FAT means much less than traditionally used in a similar dish.

OIL OPTIONAL means the recipe will work without it. The amounts recommended are all small, but do add texture and/or flavor.

TO GET MAXIMUM FLAVOR FROM THE LEAST AMOUNT OF OIL: Use flavorful oils and add them at the last minute, more like a dressing.

EXTRA VIRGIN OLIVE OIL - Use a good quality cold pressed oil in salad dressings, pasta dishes etc. where it won't be overheated. It's expensive, but is used sparingly in these recipes. A tablespoon or two can replace cupfuls in traditional recipes. If you are going to cook with high heat, use a less expensive variety. (Some studies suggest olive oil may reverse cholesterol levels).

SESAME OIL has such an intense flavor, a few drops can season a marinade or a stir-fry dish. While it is primarily used in oriental cooking, it is also great with steamed vegetables or other foods.

LIQUID VEGETABLE OILS - Most vegetable oils such as SOY, CANOLA, SUNFLOWER SEED, CORN AND OTHERS are unsaturated. Use them for baking and never to excess. The exceptions are palm or coconut oil, which are high in cholesterol and should be avoided entirely.

SAUTÉING - In this book, sautéing means to brown in a pre-heated non-stick or treated skillet. Add a tablespoon or two of water or browning sauce (if mentioned in the recipe) and cover (or stir) and cook on high heat until the juice is evaporated. Repeat if needed for that particular recipe. Add optional oil at the last minute and stir to coat.

MAYONNAISE - Traditional mayonnaise contains eggs and a lot of fat. The recipes I've seen for making soy mayonnaise are just as high in fat content, and are more work than I want to do. There are commercially-made eggless mayonnaises, but be sure to read the labels for fat content. There are some that taste good, and are comparatively low in fat. They work well on sandwiches and make a good base for Thousand Island and other dressings.

SWEETENERS

There are a number of kinds of sugar and alternative sweeteners, including many I have not tried. I will speak only from my own experience and leave any further research up to you.

FRUCTOSE is fairly equivalent to the same amount of sugar. The flavor is as sweet, but the taste response is a little slower.

APPLE JUICE CONCENTRATE - 2 tablespoons = 1 tablespoon of sugar in these recipes. Reduce the amount of liquid in the recipe to compensate. Where specifically mentioned in a recipe, it may be needed for the apple flavor. In yeast bread, it is said to improve rising.

HONEY - 1 cup = 3/4 cup sugar + 1/4 cup liquid.

MOLASSES - 1 cup = 3/4 cup sugar+ 1/4 cup liquid. Use this only when you want its distinctive flavor.

ARTIFICIAL SWEETENERS - These are totally unnecessary, but unless you are allergic to them, in moderation, they can make life more pleasant for people with blood sugar problems.

THE BLUE STUFF tastes the best. One packet is about equal to a rounded tsp. of sugar for most purposes. It will lose some of its sweetness in long cooking or high heat. For cold or stove top dishes, add at the end. For baking, you may want to use extra. It seems to work best when combined with part natural sweeteners.

THE PINK STUFF doesn't taste as much like sugar, but it fully retains its sweetness in baking. If used with some natural sweetener, it isn't too bad and does reduce calories and sugar.

STEVIA is the most natural, yet least known concentrated non-caloric sweetener. It is 100% plant derived and has been used without problems for many generations in South America and Japan. It is available in some health food stores. Stevia holds up in cooking, but does have a lingering aftertaste. If an alternate sweetener is important to you, I think you might be able to get used to it. I find it best when used to boost the sweetness of small amounts of other natural sweeteners.

VEGAN MILKS

The basic recipe for SOY MILK makes it double strength which reduces both preparation time and storage room. To use, dilute with an equal amount of water. If it is to be used full strength, it will be listed as DOUBLE MILK.

When a recipe calls for MILK or BLENDED MILK, it refers to my favorite blend of **half soy milk and half rice milk.** Soy milk is creamy but not sweet enough and rice milk is thin, lower in fat and too sweet for soups and sauces. The two blend just right into a great tasting milk. There is a rice and soy milk blend available in some health food stores, but the homemade soy milk is much better tasting and certainly more thrifty.

DOUBLE SOY MILK FROZEN IN ICE CUBE TRAYS are approximately 2 tbsps each, therefore 2 cubes plus 1/4 cup water + 1/2 cup rice milk = 1 cup milk. The thawed soy milk may look like it has curdled, but it retains the fresh taste and when stirred up works fine in all of the recipes.

OKARA

OKARA is the pulp left behind after you've extracted the soy milk. I was delighted to discover this very interesting substance. It has many, many uses and since it is a by-product, it's like receiving a bonus. Okara is rich in fiber and is higher in protein, calcium, and potassium than soy milk. To start with, it makes a good burger or sausage patty (see recipe page 46) or can be used to extend your favorite burger recipe or mix. Okara can add fiber to yeast dough without making the bread heavy and dark. Amazingly enough, this interesting substance also acts as an egg substitute in muffins and pancakes.

Freeze the okara in ice cube trays, pop out, and put in ziplock bags for future use. The average cube is approximately 2 tbsps 2 cubes equal approximately 1/4 cup (close enough for these recipes). All okara measurements in the recipes are packed down. Eggs can be used in any of the baking recipes instead of 1/4 cup okara.

VEGETABLE BROTHS

Broth or stock of some kind is an important part of good food. If you've depended on meat for this purpose all of your life, it takes some effort to find new ways. Homemade vegetable broth is usually best. It can be made and frozen (see recipe page 59). Canned Vegetable Broth is very good, and easy too. There is a huge variety of powdered vegetarian broths, bouillons, etc. However, it's important to read the labels to see if they fit your personal criteria. Perhaps the simplest broth base is soy sauce or miso. It's all a matter of preference. I personally use lite soy sauce which has less salt.

SOY SAUCE - There are many kinds of soy sauce. People sometimes prefer one over another for a variety of reasons. The differences are usually in the processing and in the ingredients. Most soy sauces are brewed and contain small amounts of wheat or preservatives and the amount of salt varies. There is soy sauce that is not brewed and contains just soybeans and water. Lots of information is available if you are interested in learning more about this subject. In making these recipes I have used a lite soy sauce which has about half the usual amount of salt.

MISO is a fermented paste made of soybeans and/or grains. It is flavorful, rich in nutrients and is considered a digestive aid. You have probably had it many times in oriental restaurants as a base for soups and sauces. There are many kinds available, ranging from mellow miso made from grain and soy combination to pure soy miso, which is the richest and darkest. When dissolved in water it can be used almost interchangeably with soy sauce. It's worth exploring to discover your favorites.

THICKENERS

Thickeners are what makes GRAVY OR SAUCE out of seasoned broth or milk. Traditionally there is a lot of animal fat involved. My recipes call for flour, cornstarch or potato flour for thickening. Rice flour and arrowroot work, too.

FLOUR can be used as a thickener in two basic ways. It can be mixed with cold fluid in the blender before it is added to the broth or milk. There is a product called WONDRA FLOUR that can be sprinkled directly into hot liquid. It's fine for some things, but not for cream sauces that require browning for flavor.

CORNSTARCH, ARROWROOT and POTATO STARCH act in a similar way. They need to be dissolved in cold water first. RICE FLOUR and POTATO FLOUR can be sprinkled directly into the hot liquid. One or two tbsps of any of these will thicken about a cup of hot liquid, depending upon how thick you want it. When making the sauce directly in the pan, such as in stir-fry, add a little of the mixture at a time until you get the desired sauce.

In baking, cornstarch added to flour makes it more like cake flour.

POTATO FLOUR is used in some recipes. It is made from the whole potato and when mixed into warm mixtures, such as loaves or patties, it makes a good binder and helps them hold their shape. Instant mashed potato flakes can also be used this same way.

VEGETARIAN GELATINS that contain no animal products can be found at most health food stores. There are packaged Kosher Gelatins that can be used for molded desserts and for thickening salad dressings.

AGAR-AGAR is a gel derived from a sea vegetable. It is widely used in home cooking and commercial products. It is beneficial to the digestive tract and is rich in vitamins and minerals. When used in cooking, it gels with or without refrigeration. Agar-agar comes in several forms including powder, flakes and sticks. For thickening 1 cup of liquid, it takes 1 to 1 1/4 tsps of flakes, but only 1/4 to 1/3 tsp of the powder.

For the pudding recipes in this book, powdered agar-agar works best. The flakes and sticks do not dissolve well in the vegan milks. Not all health food stores carry powdered agar-agar. I've found it most often in the bulk foods department. While it may seem expensive, an ounce or two goes a long, long way. Finding a place you can buy powdered agar-agar is well worth a little persistence.

CARAGEENAN is another sea vegetable product with great nutritional properties. I've never used it in cooking, but when I see it on a label, I'm glad to know it's a good natural additive.

SEASONINGS AND FLAVOR ENHANCERS

When you no longer choose to use meat to flavor your food, seasonings and other means of enhancing flavor become more important. Here are some tips on how to get the most flavor in vegan cooking. The last section of the book will have suggestions for foods that go with these soy based recipes to complete a meal, what to keep in the cupboard and freezer, and some quick meal suggestions. You may want to read it first, before you check out the recipes.

We all tend to use just a few favorite seasonings on everything. When trying a new recipe for the first time, I suggest that you obtain and try the recommended spices. YOU MAY BE PLEASANTLY SURPRISED and discover a whole new flavor combination you'll want to use in other things. My perpetual favorites are vanilla if it's sweet and garlic if it's not.

VANILLA POWDER - I get on my soap box about this. I've been using it for several years, but most people have never heard of it. It's available in most large supermarkets and in some health food stores. The advantage is that you can sprinkle it on and in many things you could never flavor with drops of liquid vanilla. My favorites are cinnamon toast, waffles, pancakes, cereal, popcorn, and in coffee. Try it. You'll like it.

FRESH GARLIC, ONIONS AND GINGER are like a holy trinity in the world of cooking. They are one group of foods dear to health and nutrition conscious people and professional chefs alike. I've included some tips that may help in the preparation and storage of these foods.

There are chopped, bottled versions of all three that are very convenient, however, they do contain preservatives. The dried, flaked or powdered versions of all three have their place in cooking, and are recommended in some of the recipes.

GARLIC -A chef's trick for preparing garlic for chopping is to smash the whole clove with the flat side of a cleaver or knife. This makes the skin very easy to remove with a minimum of handling.

A really good GARLIC PRESS, as described under utensils (pg 3), is fast and easy.

ONIONS - For minimum eye irritation while cutting onions, a sharp knife and a slight slicing motion minimizes crushing and produces less of the irritant. After chopping onions to be served raw, rinse them in cold water and pat dry to make them less pungent.

A small amount of chopped raw onion put through the GARLIC PRESS will produce onion juice and pulp that is great for subtle, evenly dispersed flavor in salad dressings, marinades etc.

GINGER - To keep fresh ginger available, I have two suggestions. Cut the ginger root into chunks and put in a small jar. Cover with wine and refrigerate. This will stay good almost indefinitely and the GARLIC PRESS works very nicely on the ginger chunks. The flavored wine is good for cooking as well.

A second method is to grate or chop the ginger root and put it in a plastic storage bag, squeezing out as much air as possible. Lay the bag flat and pat the ginger into a thin layer 1/4" thick and freeze. When you want some fresh ginger, it is easy to break off an appropriate piece without thawing the rest.

VINEGAR - Vinegar is a great flavor enhancer on salad, cooked greens and other vegetables as well as in marinades and sauces. The recipes in this book usually call for specific vinegars. I hope you try them even if they are unfamiliar. Balsamic Vinegar may seem expensive for a book on thrifty food, but the amounts used are small. It comes in a wide range of prices. Pick the best one you can afford. There are many other interesting vinegars to choose from if you don't like the ones I've suggested.

PARSLEY - Don't overlook this NUTRITIONAL AND FLAVORFUL POWER HOUSE. You may not like it's taste raw, but it is loaded with potassium and Vitamin A . When it's cooked it adds a lot of good flavor to many things. I wouldn't think of making vegetable broth, stew, soup or pasta dishes without it.

ALL OF MY RECIPES HAVE SALT OPTIONAL. The amounts suggested are consistently less than those found in most restaurants or in precooked packaged foods.

NUMEROUS STUDIES SHOW THAT PEOPLE WILL USE LESS SALT IF IT IS APPLIED AT THE TABLE.

TOASTING AND ROASTING is an important FLAVOR BOOSTER. Traditionally recipes calling for this process use oil, but grains and nuts can be toasted or roasted BY STIRRING IN A DRY SKILLET ON TOP OF THE STOVE, OR BAKED IN AN OVEN, STIRRING OCCASIONALLY UNTIL BROWN. Almonds and cashews can be roasted and chopped and put in a jar, ready for an instant garnish. Vegetables can be roasted, too, for a slightly different flavor. Roasted tomatoes are sometimes used for salsas and sauces.

HERBS AND SPICES

There is an important difference between fresh and dried herbs. They taste completely different and are not always interchangeable.

Fresh basil, for instance, is essential for pesto, which can't be made with the dried herb. If you decide to substitute fresh for dried herbs, it can be delightful to experiment with.

IT TAKES A LOT MORE OF THE FRESH HERBS, BECAUSE THEY ARE NOT AS CONCENTRATED. TOAST DRIED HERBS IN THE SKILLET to freshen and bring out more of the flavor, when you are sautéing.

FOR LONG COOKING SAUCES, STEWS, ETC., put part of the herbs in at the beginning. Taste and add more herbs near the end of the cooking. CANNED OR BOTTLED MARINARA SAUCE may be great when it goes in the jar, but it loses something along the way. It can be perked up with A LITTLE ADDED GARLIC, BASIL OR OREGANO.

A final word, don't be afraid to try other herbs and spices you read about. They can make the difference between a good cook and a mediocre one.

Chapter Three
THE SOYBEAN

"In my opinion, one of the healthiest dietary changes people can make is to substitute soy foods for some (or all) of the animal foods they now eat." Dr. Andrew Weil, Director of the Program of Integrative Medicine at the University of Arizona.

When I switched to a vegan diet, I found very few prepackaged foods that met my criteria of tastiness, healthfulness and thriftiness. Commercial soy products have important nutritional qualities, but I didn't care much for them.

Then I found a health food store that sold really good tofu. It was firm and fresh, locally made and stored in the refrigerated case in a pan covered with fresh water. This is quite a different product than the tofu that comes sealed in plastic, covered with stale water for who knows how long, that is found in most grocery stores. It is often placed in the fresh vegetable section instead of being in a refrigerated case.

I set about happily inventing interesting ways to use this good tofu. One time the health food store ran out of it and didn't expect more for several days. I didn't want to wait. I invested in a pound of soybeans (less than a dollar). I managed to find an old book I'd tucked away somewhere that told how to make soy milk and tofu. The tofu was as good as the professionally made and the soy milk was better than any I'd tried. Remember, I'm not an expert and I've not tried every variety of tofu out there. I speak only from my own experience. If you buy packaged tofu, when you get home, rinse it well and store it in fresh water.

Up until that time I had been using rice milk. It was good on cereal and other things, but was too sweet and thin bodied for the milk-based soups and sauces and casseroles I was fond of eating. The soy milk was richer tasting, but was not sweet enough to taste like regular milk. I found that they blended to make a great milk for cooking and a whole group of favorite foods was restored to me.

The other great thing I discovered from making soy milk was that the mash left over is called okara and it is an interesting, nutritious food. This piqued my curiosity and I came up with some great uses for it.

MAKING SOY MILK AND OKARA

This recipe makes double strength milk, which saves a lot of cooking time as well as storage space in the refrigerator and the freezer. At first it may seem like a lot of trouble to figure out the best set up, but with repetition, it will become almost automatic. You will need a large 8 to 10 quart kettle, a large colander that will fit in a large pan (a dish pan will do), and a 24" square of nylon organdy or thin muslin cloth. The organdy is more expensive, but greatly reduces the time it takes to extract the milk.

1 lb. dry soy beans (2 1/2 cups)
water for soaking
14 cups water (7 cups cold and 7 cups hot)

1. Wash soybeans. Put in large pot. Cover with water a few inches over the top. Soak at least 10 hours. There will be approximately 5 cups when soaked. Rinse in hot water and drain.

2. Put 2 cups of the 7 cups of cold water in an 8 to 10 quart kettle, and put over medium heat.

3. Measure out the 7 cups of hot water. Combine 1 1/2 cups of hot water and 1 1/2 cups of soaked beans in a blender or food processor. Chop until bean pieces are about like coarse corn meal. Add to the kettle on the stove. Repeat until all of the beans are in the pot.

4. Add any remaining hot water and bring to a full boil (not too fast, it can easily boil over). Stir the bottom with a pancake turner occasionally to prevent scorching. Reduce the heat and simmer for 20 to 30 minutes.

5. While the mash is cooking, place a colander over a large pan. Thoroughly rinse the organdy or thin muslin cloth and line the colander. Clip on with clothespins if needed.

6. When the mash is cooked, pour into the cloth lined colander over the large pan. Pour remaining 5 cups of cold water through the mash, a little at a time, stirring to cool and rinse the pulp.

7. When it's cool enough to handle, gather the edges of the cloth together and twist and knead until the milk is squeezed out leaving the pulp dry and crumbly. This remaining fiber is called okara. It is rich in nutrients and has some excellent uses.

You now have 3 1/2 quarts of double strength soy milk which can be bottled and refrigerated, frozen in ice cube trays for future cooking, or used to make tofu.

MAKING TOFU

Tofu is an important staple to vegans because it is a nutritionally good source of complete protein, calcium and other nutrients. It complements grains and nuts, making a protein rich diet possible without animal products. It is also very digestible because the solidifier and troublesome part of the bean goes down the drain with the whey.

You can use the same kettle and cloth used to make the soy milk. You will need a small strainer to act as a mold, a lid slightly smaller than the strainer (it does not have to fit exactly), and a 1 pound weight to compress the lid. I use a jar of water or a large can of food.

TOFU

3 1/2 quarts double strength soy milk
2 tsps Epsom salts (solidifier)
1 1/2 cups warm water

1. Return the double strength soy milk to the kettle and bring to a boil slowly, stirring occasionally with a pancake turner to prevent burning.

2. While it is heating, select a small strainer to act as a mold. Line it with nylon organdy or wet muslin cloth. Find a lid of some kind that is slightly smaller than the mold. Select a one pound weight. A large can of food will do.

3. To prepare the solidifier, add the Epsom salts to the warm water. Stir until dissolved and set aside. (Amounts needed will vary with local water. Filtered water works best).

4. When soy milk boils, remove from heat. Gently mix in approximately 1/3 of solidifier. Add another 1/3 and stop the agitation by drawing spoon gently through the milk until the motion stops. Let stand three minutes. If mixture has not curdled add more solidifier. Whey should be fairly clear. Throw away any remaining solidifier.

5. Ladle curds gently into mold. Work slowly letting the whey drain away. Fold the cloth over curds. Cover with the lid that is slightly smaller than the mold. Weight with a one pound can or jar of water. Allow to stand for about 25 minutes, cooling in the mold. Then lift from the mold and immerse in cold water.

6. When cool, carefully remove the tofu from the cloth. Rinse and store, covered with water. Fresh tofu will keep for several weeks in the refrigerator if you rinse and put in fresh water every other day.
One pound of soy beans makes about 14 oz of tofu.

PART TWO - COOKING WITH SOY MILK

Some of the things I most missed when I no longer used dairy products were potato soup, scalloped potatoes, white sauce, and milk gravy. They were such an integral part of the country cooking I enjoy. My first experiments with soy milk were disappointing. I'd already observed that rice milk was delicious for cereal, but too sweet for soups and sauces. Then I discovered that the creamy flavor of fresh soy milk, when blended with rice milk, (approximately 1/2 and 1/2) tasted just right for cooking many of my old favorites. I've certainly not tried all forms of soy milk. I'm sure there are some that would work well with these recipes. Nevertheless, fresh made soy milk is awfully good and is a fraction of the cost of any other liquid soy milk I've seen. The recipes in this chapter are also designed to contain little or no added fat.

Chapter Four
SAUCES

WHITE SAUCE OR COUNTRY GRAVY

There are two basic differences between white sauce and country gravy. White sauce is made with a rue of butter or margarine with flour cooked in it, but not browned. Then milk is added and stirred until it is smooth and thick. Gravy is usually made with meat drippings and the flour is browned in the fat before adding milk. I've discovered a fairly good way to make both of these sauces without fat. I will include recipes for low fat versions which admittedly taste a bit better. EITHER OF THESE RECIPES CAN BE USED IN CASSEROLES AND OTHER RECIPES CALLING FOR CONVENTIONAL WHITE SAUCE. A time saving tip: brown extra flour and store in a jar ready for immediate use.

NON-FAT WHITE SAUCE OR GRAVY

1/2 cup unbleached flour
2 cups blended milk (soy and rice)
1/4 tsp salt (optional)
Pepper to taste

Heat a skillet on medium heat. Add the dry flour, stir and cook. For white sauce, remove from the heat when it starts to show a tinge of brown. For gravy, let it brown until it's the color of coffee with cream. Let it cool slightly. Place the milk and the cooked flour in a blender and mix until smooth. Pour the mixture back into the skillet and stir until it thickens. Add salt and pepper and other seasonings to taste. This will be ready to use in any recipe calling for a thick white sauce. Add more milk for a thinner sauce or for cream soups.

LOW-FAT WHITE SAUCE OR GRAVY

This has the good browned flavor of traditional sauce or gravy, with about a fourth of the fat.

2 tsps oil or margarine
Plus the same ingredients as above
Mix 2 tbsps of the flour and the milk in a blender. Set aside. Heat the oil or margarine in a skillet. Add the remaining 2 tbsp of flour and stir until it browns. Add the milk and flour mixture and stir immediately with a fork. Keep stirring until it thickens.

COUNTRY SAUSAGE GRAVY

This can be made with okara sausage bits or patties (see recipe page 46) Your favorite veggieburger might be good prepared this way as well.

Brown the sausage in a non-stick skillet. As in the recipe for low fat gravy, add 2 tsps margarine or oil, 2 tbsp flour. Stir until flour is brown. Then add 1 cup of milk blend mixed with remaining flour (see thickening alternatives). Stir until gravy thickens. Add extra milk for thinner gravy. Serve over low-fat biscuits or mashed potatoes.

CHEEZEE SAUCE

1 cup white sauce
1/2 cup soy whiz (see recipe page 35)
Stir together white sauce and soy whiz. Use on anything where you would ordinarily use a cheese sauce. It's especially nice with vegetable crepes, casseroles, etc.

Chapter Five
CREAM SOUPS AND MORE

All of the soups in this next group have unique, individual flavoring, yet each one is seasoned very simply. The first two recipes are among the quickest in the book and are made from ingredients you usually have on hand. It's important to have all of the ingredients measured and ready before you start. The last two recipes in this section are good hot in the winter or cold in summer.

QUICK CORN CHOWDER

1 tbsp dry onion flakes
1 1/2 cups blended milk
1 16 oz can cream style corn
1/2 cup mashed potato flakes
Salt, pepper and margarine if desired.

Have the milk measured and the can of corn open. Heat a medium saucepan slightly and add onion flakes. Toast until they are brown, then quickly add the milk, corn and potato flakes. Heat, taste, season if desired, and serve.
Makes two large bowls.

OLD FASHIONED TOMATO SOUP

This is possibly the quickest and easiest recipe in this book.

Put one can of diced tomatoes in a sauce pan and bring to a boil. Add a pinch of baking soda and stir a little. Then add a cup or two of blended milk. Reheat, salt and pepper to taste and serve.

CREAM OF POTATO SOUP

1 cup peeled and diced potatoes
1 stalk celery, diced
2 sprigs of parsley, chopped
3/4 cup water
1/2 tsp salt (optional)
1/2 onion, diced
2 vegetarian breakfast strips, diced (optional)

1 tbsp oil or margarine
2 tbsps flour
2 cups or more of blended milk
1 tsp garlic powder
1 tsp onion powder
1/2 tsp thyme (this makes it for me)
Salt and pepper to taste.

Cook the potatoes, celery and parsley in the salted water until they are tender (the microwave is fast for this). Brown the breakfast strips in non-stick skillet until crisp. Add onions and brown until translucent in 1/2 of the oil or margarine. Add the remaining margarine and the flour. Stir and cook for a minute then add 1/2 the milk and stir until it thickens. Add to the cooked vegetables along with the remaining milk. Season with garlic and onion powder and thyme. Heat and taste for salt and pepper. If you like it thicker, sprinkle and stir in Wondra flour, potato flour or a few instant potato flakes.

VARIATIONS: You can make other cream of vegetable soups the same way, with or without potatoes. For mushroom soup, sauté mushrooms along with the onions.

BROCCOLI SOUP

1 1/2 cups chopped broccoli (fresh or frozen)
1/2 cup water
1/2 tsp salt (optional)
2 cups blended milk
2/3 cup instant mashed potato flakes
1/2 tsp marjoram leaves

Cook the broccoli in the water until done, but still crisp (Frozen broccoli requires less time). Add the blended milk, salt and potato flakes. Sprinkle in the marjoram leaves, heat and serve.

BRUSSELS SPROUTS SOUP

This soup sounds weird, but most people won't guess what's in it. Actually it's very good.

2 cups peeled and cubed potatoes
2 cups quartered brussels sprouts
3/4 cup blended milk
1 tbsp margarine

1 tsp lemon juice
Salt and pepper to taste.

Cook the potatoes in a small amount of water until tender. At the same time, cook the Brussels sprouts separately in a little water until they are soft, but not strong flavored. Combine the potatoes and sprouts, including the water. Add the margarine, blended milk, salt and pepper. Blend all together until smooth. Stir in the lemon juice. It should be just slightly tart. Add a little more lemon if necessary. Re-heat or chill. It's good either way. Makes two large bowls.

CARROT SOUP

1/2 onion, diced
1 1/2 cups carrots, chopped (3 or 4 medium)
1 or 2 cloves fresh garlic or 1 tsp garlic powder
2 tsps minced fresh ginger
2 tsps dry mustard
1/2 tsp turmeric
1 cup water
2 cups blended milk
2 tbsps flour
1/2 tsp salt (optional)
2 tbsps orange juice concentrate
1 tbsp lemon juice
1 or 2 tsps curry powder(optional)

Sauté the onions in a non-stick skillet for two or three minutes. Add the chopped carrots, garlic, ginger, dry mustard and turmeric. Stir and brown, adding a tablespoon or two of water as needed, until the onions are translucent (3 or 4 minutes). Add the water and simmer until the carrots are soft. Cool slightly and puree`(a hand blender works well). Put in a sauce pan with the milk and flour. Blend until smooth and bring to a boil to thicken. Stir in the orange juice concentrate and lemon juice. It's great served cold or hot, with or without the curry powder. Your choice. Makes 4 cups.

SCALLOPED POTATOES

4 cups peeled sliced potatoes
1/2 chopped onion
4 tbsps flour
2 cups blended milk
1 tbsp margarine (optional)

1 tsp salt (optional)
1/4 tsp pepper (optional)
1 tsp garlic powder (optional)
Add salt and seasonings to the milk and pre-heat (this will speed up the process). Place 1/3 of the potato slices in a baking dish. Sprinkle on some chopped onion and a little of the flour. Repeat until potatoes are used up. Pour hot milk over the potatoes until it shows between the top layer of potatoes. Bake at 350º for 60 to 70 minutes. This process may be speeded up by slightly pre-cooking the whole dish in the microwave until it starts to bubble, but not boil over. (10 to 20 minutes). Finish in the oven until potatoes are well done. Dot with margarine before serving if desired. Makes 4 to 6 servings.

CREPES

Crepes are generally mostly eggs and milk, and are filled and/or topped with a lot of cheeses and cream sauces. This sounds impossible for a vegan, however, I've come up with recipes that work very well. Crepes offer such a variety of possibilities. They're one of those things that can be made with whatever vegetables or fruits you have on hand. They can be a terrific addition to any menu.

The pancake:
1 cup soy double strength milk
2 tsps vegetable oil
1/2 cup whole wheat flour
1/4 tsp salt (optional)

Blend ingredients together in blender. Batter should be very thin. Let stand while you're preparing fillings. Heat a well treated griddle on medium heat. Test a small amount to test pan and batter. Pour a tablespoon or two of batter on to the griddle and turn pan to spread as thin as possible. Brown really well until firm. Loosen all of the edges with the spatula to see if it will hold together and when you think it's ready, turn over and brown the other side. Adjust the batter for thickness or thinness. This all will take some practice, but once you get it right it's easier next time. Crepes can be made in advance and reheated.

Vegetable dinner crepes: Have ready finely chopped steamed or sautéed vegetables such as spinach, mushrooms, broccoli, cauliflower, zucchini, eggplant and onions, or asparagus.
Have ready white sauce (with sautéed onions, mushrooms or favorite herbs added), soy whiz, cheezee sauce, soy ricotta or marinara sauce.

Garnishes: toasted sesame seed, chopped nuts, chopped green onions, bacon bits or fresh herbs.

Fill each crepe with a little sauce and vegetables. Roll it up and place with edges down on a plate. Cover with more sauce and garnish if desired. Fillings and sauces should be warm or the entire crepe can be heated for a minute in the microwave before serving.

Suggested combinations:

Cannelloni crepes: Put a little marinara sauce on the crepe. Fill with tofu ricotta and steamed spinach. Top generously with marinara sauce.

Artichoke hearts: Fill crepe with soy whiz and artichoke hearts. Top with cheezee sauce. Garnish with bacon bits.
Try sautéed zucchini, onions and tomato slices with cheezee sauce. Top with toasted sesame seeds.

Dessert crepes: Fill with sweetened tofu ricotta and sweetened fruit. Top with pureed fruit, more tofu ricotta, or a sprinkle of powdered sugar. Fruit only jams work as well.

CREAMED NEW POTATOES AND PEAS

This recipe gives approximate measurements per serving. Multiply as needed.
1 cup potato chunks
1/3 cup water
Salt to taste
1/4 cup fresh or frozen peas
1/2 cup fat free white sauce
1 tbsp margarine (optional)

Scrub and scrape peelings from new potatoes and cut in uniform chunks. Cook in a small amount of salted water until almost done. Add 1/4 cup fresh or frozen peas and cook a few more minutes (the microwave is great for this). Stir in the white sauce. Add any desired seasonings such as pepper or thyme. Margarine added at this time will produce the maximum amount of flavor.

VARIATIONS: other vegetables can be prepared this same way, e.g. mixed vegetables and potatoes, or eggplant and onion.

Chapter Six
PUDDINGS AND PIE FILLINGS

Making good, eggless, dairy-free puddings required considerable experimentation. The soy and rice milk did not act quite like dairy milk when combined with corn starch or tapioca alone. I tried agar-agar (see page 7) by itself and found that it had a thickening effect, but was not the texture and taste of pudding. When I tested various combinations and proportions of these thickeners I was able to make some very tasty puddings and pie fillings.

CHOCOLATE PUDDING OR PIE FILLING

For a 9" pie, double the pudding recipe.

1/4 cup cocoa
1/3 cup sugar or alternatives
3/4 tsp powdered agar-agar
vanilla to taste
2 cups blended milk
pinch of salt (optional)
1/4 cup cornstarch
1 tbsp margarine (optional)

Mix the cocoa, sugar, agar-agar and vanilla in the bottom of a medium saucepan. Add 1 1/2 cups of the milk, reserving the rest for later. Bring to a boil, stirring until free of lumps. Boil slowly for 5 minutes exactly, stirring occasionally (6 minutes for pie). Dissolve the cornstarch in the reserved 1/2 cup of milk and add the mixture to the hot pudding, stirring until it returns to a boil and thickens. Remove immediately from the burner. If desired, stir in the margarine or a pinch of salt. Chill and serve. Makes 2 cups.

VARIATION: For mocha flavor, add 2 tsps instant coffee to the cornstarch mixture.

BASIC VANILLA PUDDING OR PIE FILLING

Double the recipe to fill a 9" pie shell.

1/2 tsp powdered agar-agar
1/3 cup sugar or alternatives
vanilla powder
1/4 cup cornstarch
2 cups blended milk
small pinch salt (optional)
1 tbsp margarine(optional)

In a small saucepan, combine agar-agar, sugar, vanilla powder and 1 1/2 cups of the blended milk, reserving the remaining 1/2 cup. Bring to a boil over medium high heat. Boil slowly for exactly 5 minutes (6 minutes for pie filling). Mix the cornstarch with the remaining cold milk and stir in to the hot pudding. Continue stirring until it returns to a boil and thickens. Remove from the heat immediately. Stir in margarine or salt if desired. Pour into serving dishes or pie shell. Makes 2 cups.

VARIATIONS: For BANANA CREAM PIE, slice two bananas and arrange slices to cover the bottom of a pre-baked, cooled 9" pie shell. Spoon in the slightly cooled filling and top with remaining banana slices.

For COCONUT CREAM pie, stir in 1/2 cup shredded coconut. Sprinkle a little more on top.

To make a CREAM SAUCE for topping bread pudding, baked apples or other desserts, reduce the agar-agar to 1/4 tsp and the cornstarch to 2 tbsps.

CARAMEL PUDDING OR PIE FILLING

Double the pudding recipe to fill a 9" pie crust.

1/4 cup water
1/3 to 1/2 cup sugar or fructose only
1/2 tsp powdered agar-agar
1 3/4 cups blended milk
1/4 cup corn starch
vanilla to taste
1 tbsp margarine (optional)
a pinch of salt

Put a medium saucepan on high heat. Add the sugar or fructose. Stir constantly as it melts and starts to brown. When it reaches a nice brown caramel color remove from the burner (fructose melts faster, but browns more slowly.) Add the water to the browned sugar, quickly moving away to avoid rising steam. Stir and cook until sugar is dissolved. Add 1 1/4 cups of the milk and the agar-agar, reserving the remaining 1/2 cup milk. Boil for 5 minutes exactly, stirring occasionally (6 minutes for pie).

Mix the cornstarch and vanilla with the remaining milk. Stir into the hot pudding and continue to stir until it returns to a boil and thickens. Remove from the burner immediately and pour into serving dishes (or pie shell) and chill. Makes 2 cups.

VARIATIONS: By using only 1/4 tsp powdered agar-agar and 2 tbsps corn starch, this makes a delicious CARAMEL SAUCE to use over bread puddings or other desserts.

TAPIOCA PUDDING

1/4 tsp powdered agar-agar
1/4 cup minute tapioca
1/4 to 1/3 cup sugar or alternatives
vanilla powder
2 cups blended milk
small pinch of salt (optional)
1 tbsp margarine (optional)

Mix tapioca, agar-agar powder, sweetener, vanilla and milk in a small saucepan and let stand for at least ten minutes. Bring to a boil and continue to boil for 5 minutes. Pour into serving dishes and chill. Makes 2 cups.

VARIATIONS: For a really deluxe dessert, dice 2 cups fresh ripe peaches. Add a little sweetener and 1/4 tsp ground cloves. Let stand while you make and chill 1 recipe of tapioca pudding.
Alternate layers of peaches and pudding in stemmed glasses. Chill and serve. Try other fruits and berries in season.

CREAMY RICE PUDDING

This recipe for rice pudding is very simple and natural. It requires neither thickening nor sweetening, and has no added fat, yet it makes a creamy, delicious, breakfast or dessert.

1/2 cup short grain brown rice
1/2 cup water
2 cups blended milk
vanilla to taste
1/2 tsp cinnamon (optional)
1/4 cup raisins (optional)

Place rice and water in a sauce pan. Boil until most of the water is absorbed (7 to 9 minutes). Add blended milk, cinnamon, and vanilla. Return to a boil and turn down to the lowest setting. When the boil has partially subsided, cover and boil slowly until the rice is tender and the sauce is thick and creamy (about 50 minutes for brown and 20 minutes for white). This pudding requires very little attention while it's cooking. Near the end, stir in the raisins. Monitor the tenderness of the rice and the thickness of the pudding and adjust the cooking time, adding a little water or milk if necessary. If it's too soupy remove the lid and boil briskly for a few minutes until the sauce is just right. It will thicken more as it cools. Serve hot or cold for breakfast or dessert. Makes about 2 cups.

BREAD PUDDING

2 1/4 cups blended milk
1/2 tsp powdered agar-agar
1/3 to 1/2 cup fructose, sugar or alternatives
vanilla to taste
1 tsp cinnamon
1/4 tsp nutmeg (optional)
2 cups stale or lightly toasted bread cubes
1/4 cup raisins and/or nuts to taste (optional)

Place milk, agar-agar, sweetening and spices in a saucepan. Bring to a boil and cook for 5 minutes. Stir in bread cubes, raisins and nuts. Chill to thicken. Makes 2 cups.

VARIATIONS: An equal amount of cooked rice can be substituted for the bread cubes.

PUMPKIN PIE

This pie may be made with pureed winter squash or sweet potatoes as well. Adjust the sweetness to taste. You can use either the fat-free option described in the recipe or a pastry or crumb crust. (Be aware that store bought crusts frequently contain lard.)

2 1/4 cups blended milk
1/2 cup brown sugar or alternatives
1 1/4 tsp powdered agar-agar
1 1/2 to 2 tsps pumpkin pie spice
1 3/4 cup cooked, pureed pumpkin (15 oz can)
1 tbsp corn starch
vanilla to taste
1/4 tsp salt (optional)
1/3 cup corn flake crumbs or a 9" cooked crust

Set aside 1/4 cup of the blended milk. Put the remaining 2 cups in a saucepan with the sweetener, agar-agar and seasonings. Bring to a boil and cook exactly 5 minutes. Stir in the pumpkin and mix until smooth. Combine the cornstarch with the remaining milk and add to the pumpkin mixture. Return to a boil. When it thickens, remove from the stove quickly. Let cool slightly. Spoon into a prepared crust or use the fat-free option, as follows: wet a 9" pie plate and lightly towel dry, leaving some moisture. Sprinkle the corn flake crumbs in the bottom and tilt to get some of the crumbs to stick to the sides (though not a crust, is surprisingly tasty). Carefully spoon the filling into the pie pan to avoid disturbing the crumbs. Smooth the top, then garnish with more crumbs and chill.

Chapter Seven
BEVERAGES

These are some of my favorite blended milk drinks. The more hearty ones make a great breakfast or lunch, while others are good treats for any occasion. Careful blending and tasting of the milks is a major factor in making these drinks delightfully satisfying.

BANANA NOG

Selecting nice, ripe fruit and using just the right touch of spices makes these very special. For those of us who find few things we can eat or drink at most holiday parties, this one is good to make and take along.

Blend until smooth: 1 banana, a cup blended milk and some powdered vanilla. Add some rum extract or actual rum if you'd like. Top with a sprinkle of freshly ground nutmeg. For my taste this needs no additional sweetening.

In season, any number of fresh ripe fruits may be used instead of or in addition to bananas. My favorites are peaches with a touch of cloves, apples with cinnamon, or fresh berries of any kind.

For breakfast or lunch blend in 1/4 cup crumbled tofu.

OLD FASHIONED HOT COCOA

Some heart healthy diet regimens include cocoa powder. If this is not for you, carob powder may be substituted.

1 tbsp cocoa powder (or carob)
2 or 3 tsp sugar or alternatives
powdered vanilla
2 tbsp hot water
1 cup blended milk

Mix the cocoa, sugar and vanilla in the bottom of a large mug. Add the hot water and stir until smooth. Next add the milk and then microwave until nice and hot (about 1 1/2 minutes). Stir and serve.

CAFE` AU LAIT

Cafe` au lait usually consists of equal parts of strong coffee and hot milk. Right now, there are many popular ways combining the two. It's possible to make delicious drinks that are neither "cafe`" nor "au lait".

In some health food stores, there are organic coffees in regular or decaf. When combined with blended soy and rice milk, a sprinkle of vanilla, sweetener, and/or your favorite spice, they make a delicious treat.

The roasted soybean coffee (page 61) used in this manner can also be tasty and satisfying. You may want to try other non-coffee beverages as well, until you find your favorite combinations. I like them hot in winter and chilled in summer. These beverages are nice to take along to a party or a picnic.

In general, the method is to make your coffee, cereal beverage etc. extra strong. Then add your choice of blended milks (almond milk is nice), vanilla, spices and sweeteners until it tastes just right. Microwave until hot, or chill until cold.

PART THREE - COOKING WITH TOFU

"... tofu is an extremely versatile food, but you cannot take it home, dump it into a salad, and expect your family to like it. With a little ingenuity and effort, it can be turned into delicious main dishes, spreads, even desserts that do not seem strange at all." Dr. Andrew Weil, Director of the Program of Integrative Medicine at the University of Arizona.

There are three primary ways to cook with tofu. Each of them work in an endless number of recipes.

SLICED, CUBED OR CRUMBLED TOFU: can be marinated with many different sauces and used in numerous recipes such as stir fry, pasta dishes, chili and more.

FROZEN TOFU: has a completely different texture when thawed. It becomes porous and sponge like. It works great when you need firmness, such as on kabobs (see recipe page 33). When the moisture is squeezed out, it absorbs flavors well and can be crumbled and added to any number of foods. Freezing is a good way to keep a back-up supply on hand. Pre-cooked things like baked tofu, soy whiz, and stuffed buns are as good or better after freezing.

WHIPPED TOFU: has a texture somewhat like ricotta cheese and with the right flavoring is very versatile. It also makes a good ingredient in loaves, casseroles, etc.

This section will contain recipes for all of these ways of preparing tofu. Each one has many possible off-shoots, if you care to use your imagination.

Chapter Six
SLICED, CUBED OR CRUMBLED

BAKED TOFU

I call baked tofu "My Baloney" because it is easy to keep on hand for sandwiches or any other thing where you would use cold cuts. I sometimes take it to barbecues to be warmed on the grill. My favorite sandwich for traveling is baked tofu on a homemade bun with mustard, relish and dill pickles. It's good hot, too, with mashed potatoes and gravy. Freezing after baking actually improves it, in my opinion, but it's good fresh as well and keeps a week or two in the refrigerator.

1/4 cup lite soy sauce
1/2 tsp minced ginger
1 tsp garlic powder
1/4 tsp liquid smoke (optional)
A block of firm fresh tofu

Mix together every thing but the tofu and pour it in a flat, non-stick baking pan. Slice the desired amount of good firm tofu in 1/4 inch slices and lay in the sauce in the pan. Turn over to coat the other side. Bake in a pre-heated oven at 325º for 30 minutes, turn and bake 30 minutes more. Baking time will vary with moisture of the tofu. When done it should be brown and firm without burning the sauce.

VARIATIONS: Add pepper or other hot spices to basic sauce. Substitute teriyaki sauce, barbecue sauce or whatever you'd like.

ROASTED VEGETABLES AND TOFU

Roasting brings out the flavor of vegetables in a unique way. It is one of the easiest most adaptable ways to prepare them and requires little attention while it's cooking. You can use whatever you have on hand. The tofu blends in well and makes it a hearty dish. I'm giving two combinations I especially like, but this is more of a method than a recipe.

Cut firm tofu into chunks, as well as several of the following: potatoes - skins and all, onions - cut in quarters, green pepper, carrots, celery stalks, zucchini, small whole tomatoes or any other seasonal veggies.

1 or 2 tsps olive oil
Any of the following: seasoned salt, lemon pepper, garlic powder or your favorite soup base. Put all of the veggies in a large bowl. Add just enough oil to barely coat the vegetables and make the seasonings stick. It takes very little. You can use non-stick spray instead if you'd like. Spread out in a flat pan so they're just one layer deep. Bake in a pre-heated oven at 375º until tender and browned. Usually about 45 minutes.

VARIATION: A favorite combination is yams, apple slices (with skin), tofu cubes and pecans. Sprinkle with vegetable oil, 2 tablespoons of apple juice concentrate and some garam masala (see recipe page 32) or curry powder. Bake until done, stirring a few times (approximately 45 minutes at 350º.)

BRAISED TOFU WITH STIR FRY VEGETABLES

Stir-fry lends itself well to low fat cooking. it can be prepared with or without oil. In Chinese food it is important to cut all of the vegetables in a particular dish a similar size for even cooking. BE VERY CAREFUL NOT TO OVERCOOK BY EVEN A FEW SECONDS. I prefer an iron skillet for low-fat stir-fry.

Marinade
1/2 cup tofu cubes
1/2 cup soy sauce + 2 tbsp apple juice concentrate (or 1/2 cup teriyaki sauce)
1/2 tsp each minced ginger and garlic
1/4 tsp sesame oil
4 or 5 cups chopped vegetables
1/2 cup water
2 tbsps corn starch dissolved in 1/2 cup water

Slice the tofu in 1/2 inch slices. Cut slices in about 1 inch squares and put in plastic bowl with lid. Mix the marinade and pour over the tofu cubes. Marinate while you're preparing the vegetables, turning the bowl over a time or two to distribute flavors.

It's important to pick out a main vegetable and several secondary vegetables. My most common main veggies are bean sprouts, asparagus, broccoli, Chinese long beans or cabbage. My favorite secondary vegetables are onions (almost mandatory), celery, green pepper, pea pods, bok choy and carrots. Canned water chestnuts and bamboo shoots are good too. The vegetables should be fairly uniform in size for more even cooking, e.g. chop finer to go with bean sprouts.

Have all of the ingredients prepared and within easy reach. Don't forget the cornstarch and water mixture and some plain water. Preheat skillet (non-stick sprayed or with a little sesame oil) until very hot. It's important to maintain high heat throughout. Remove tofu cubes from the marinade and brown quickly, stirring to brown all sides. This will take no more than a minute. Put in the vegetables and add the marinade. Stir a few minutes, adding a little water to keep moist. The vegetables should be barely hot through and wilted a little. **It's very important not to overcook.** Speed is extra critical when using bean sprouts, because of their size. Finish by adding some of the cornstarch and water thickening when they're barely heated through. Add more cornstarch or more plain water or soy sauce until the sauce is the right thickness. It should coat the vegetables without being either too soupy or too dry. Remove from the heat immediately. Serve over rice, noodles or with bean threads. Top with toasted almonds or cashews and/or chopped green onion tops.

Tofu, marinated as in the previous recipe, can be used in several ways. It's good cold from the refrigerator. Put it on a plate with some toothpicks and you have hors d'oeuvres. A favorite is my adaptation of Chinese chicken salad. This recipe serves several people generously.

CHINESE TOFU SALAD WITH PEANUT SAUCE

Marinade
1/2 cup soy sauce +2 tbsp apple juice concentrate (or 1/2 cup teriyaki sauce)
1/2 tsp each, minced ginger and garlic
1/4/tsp sesame oil
1 tbsp rice vinegar or white vinegar
1/2 cup diced tofu

Combine tofu, marinade and vinegar in a lidded bowl. Set aside while fixing the rest of the ingredients, turning over a few times to coat all sides.

Peanut Sauce
1/4 cup fresh cilantro - finely chopped
1/4 cup green onions - finely chopped
1/2 cup rice vinegar or white vinegar
1/4 cup sugar or alternatives
1/2 cup soy sauce
2 tbsps sesame oil
3/4 cup peanut butter
1/4 to 1 tsp Szechwan hot sauce or red pepper

Blend all of the ingredients together until smooth. At first, add only a small amount of hot sauce. Taste and adjust to your taste. If the sauce is too thin, add a little extra peanut butter.
This will be enough for several salads and will keep a long time if refrigerated.

The Salad
3 or 4 cups coarsely shredded cabbage
Some snowpeas, broken in thirds

2 or 3 chopped green onions
1 package ramen noodles - crumbled (optional)
2 tbsp toasted sesame seeds
1/3 cup toasted cashews or almonds.

Crumble ramen in the bottom of a large bowl (optional). Add the cabbage, snowpeas and onions. Pour tofu and marinade into the bowl and toss to coat. Top with sesame seeds, cashews and a drizzle of peanut sauce. Serve with extra peanut sauce on the side for those who want more.

TOFU FRIED RICE

1 cup long grain white or brown rice
1 3/4 cups water
1/2 tsp sesame oil
1/2 cup crumbled tofu
4 finely chopped green onions, tops and all
1/3 cup finely chopped celery, mushrooms, water chestnuts and/or peas (optional)
Lite soy sauce to taste
Toasted almonds or cashew pieces (optional)

Combine rice and water in a sauce pan. Bring to a boil, cooking uncovered a few minutes until some of the water is absorbed. Turn the burner down very low. Cover and cook 1/2 hour for white rice, 45 minutes for brown. Rice should be tender, fluffy and dry. Pre-heat a non stick coated skillet until very hot. Put in sesame oil. Add crumbled tofu and vegetables, reserving some green onion tops to garnish. Stir and cook for a minute or two. Add some soy sauce, stir quickly and add rice. Stir and cook until ingredients are well mixed and rice is hot. Taste for soy sauce and add more if needed. Garnish with green onions and toasted nuts.

MEDITERRANEAN TOFU AND
EGGPLANT CURRY

This can be made with either eggplant or tofu or both. I had this dish at a restaurant and had no idea what the seasoning was. I really liked it. I knew it was not like the curries I had tasted before. I stumbled across a blend of seasonings that tasted just like the restaurant dish I liked so well. I found out it is called garam masala. I've included the recipe. I use it in other recipes as an alternative seasoning.

2 or 3 cups cooked basmati rice
1 cup bite-sized tofu pieces
1/2 eggplant sliced

Marinade: 1 tbsp apple juice concentrate, 1 tbsp water, 1 tbsp soy sauce, 1/4 tsp garam masala, 1 tbsp olive oil (optional)

Sauce: 1 can chopped or crushed tomatoes
1/2 onion - chopped
1/2 cup mushrooms - coarsely chopped (optional)
1/2 cup celery - chopped
1 apple - chopped
1 small carrot - chopped
1/4 cup apple juice concentrate
2 tsps garam masala or curry powder

Put the rice on to cook. Slice eggplant and cut tofu in 1/2 inch slices and cut into bite sized pieces. Mix the marinade and pour over egg-plant and tofu, tossing to coat. Set aside.

Sauté onions in a heavy non-stick skillet until golden brown. Add the mushrooms, celery, apples and carrots and continue to stir for about a minute. Put in apple juice concentrate and seasonings. Cook on high heat, reducing the juice until it caramelizes slightly. Add toma-toes, reduce heat and simmer for ten minutes. If you want it hotter, add more seasoning to taste.

Grill eggplant slices until tender. Grill tofu until brown on both sides. Put eggplant slices and tofu chunks on the plate with rice on the side. Top with the sauce and serve.

GARAM MASALA

All ingredients are ground. Put in a small jar, mix well and keep for future use.
3 tsp. cumin
3/4 tsp black pepper (more if you like it hot)
2 tbsp coriander
1 1/2 tsp each, cloves and cinnamon

BARBECUED TOFU KABOBS

These kabobs make a festive and colorful party dish. They can be grilled outdoors or cooked under the broiler. If you'd like, guests can put their own together to suit their individual tastes. This is especially nice if your guests are a mixture of vegans and meat eaters.

Previously frozen tofu
Onion slices
Mushrooms
Pineapple chunks
Squash chunks
Tomatoes quartered
Other fruits or vegetables
Skewers
Barbecue sauce

The previously frozen tofu will be sponge-like when thawed. Gently squeeze out most of the fluid and cut in 1 inch cubes. Prepare vegetable chunks and slices of your choice. Alternate tofu and vegetables on the skewers. Brush with your favorite barbecue sauce and place on the grill. Cook a few minutes on each side, brushing on additional sauce if desired.

FAJITAS

Marinade:
1/2 cup water
1 tbsp cornstarch
1/4 cup ketchup
1 tsp garlic powder or 1 or 2 cloves fresh garlic
2 or 3 tbsps chili powder
1/2 tsp oregano (optional)
1/2 tsp salt (optional)
hot sauce to your taste (optional)
1 tbsp chopped fresh cilantro (optional)

<u>Filling:</u>
1 cup tofu cubes
1 cup onion strips (1 medium)
1 cup green or red bell pepper strips (1 medium)
1 cup tomato wedges
1 1/2 cups cooked brown rice (optional)

1 dozen corn tortillas or
6 burrito-sized wheat tortillas

Stir together the marinade ingredients. Add the tofu cubes and let stand while you're preparing the vegetables.

Heat a non-stick or treated skillet. Remove the tofu from the marinade (a slotted spoon works well). Stir and brown in a hot skillet for about two minutes. Add the onion and pepper strips, and cook and stir for about 5 minutes. Put in the tomato wedges, and a tablespoon or two of water. Cover and cook for 4 or 5 minutes more. Stir the marinade well before adding to the skillet and cook until it thickens.

Tortillas need to be hot to fold. Heat 2 or 3 minutes spread out on a cookie sheet at 350º, or wrapped loosely in a paper towel and microwaved for 1 minute.

Put a spoonful or two of the filling in a line at the center of the tortilla. Add rice if desired. Fold up the bottom first and then roll up from the side. Pick up and eat.

To re-heat later, put filling on a cold tortilla, microwave 30 seconds for corn or 1 minute for flour. Fold and eat.

Chapter Nine
WHIPPED TOFU

TOFU RICOTTA
With variations of this recipe, whipped tofu can be used almost anywhere you would use ricotta, cream cheese or even sour cream. It's great for filling and crepes (see recipe page 19).

3/4 cup crumbled tofu
1 tbsp double strength soy milk
1 tbsp rice milk
1 tbsp lemon juice
1/4 tsp salt

Whip together until very smooth. In this case the salt is important to make it taste like a soft cheese. It is best when chilled overnight as well. The flavors blend to make it more cheese-like. Tofu ricotta is very useful in vegetable crepes and desserts (see individual recipes).

Note:
1. If you want more of a sour cream taste, before using, add 1/4 teaspoon more lemon juice and let stand awhile.

2. For desserts, sweeten to taste and add vanilla. Dilute with milk for softer topping. Use to fill dessert crepes or use as a whipped topping for baked apples, gingerbread, cobbler, fruit salad or any other kind of dessert.

ORANGE TOFU SPREAD

This simple combination is great on toast or waffles, and is especially good as a topping for chocolate pudding..

Blend together
1 cup crumbled tofu
6 tbsp orange juice concentrate
Vanilla
pinch of salt (optional)

VARIATION: Whip in 6 tbsp peanut butter.

SOY WHIZ

This is probably the most versatile food in this book. It is definitely a staple at my house. You will find recipes in all sections of this book which put it to use. Because of this a friend dubbed it "Soy Whiz" and the name has stuck.

I originally made this from a recipe which used fresh-made soy milk, kept at room temperature a few days until it soured. The process required several days and started out with 5 lbs of raw peanut butter, gallons of soy milk and hours of cooking. My version tastes every bit as good and is much quicker.

All measurements are approximate and can be varied according to taste without harming the outcome.

1 cup raw nuts or seeds (I like sunflower seeds.)

1 cup tomato sauce
1 1/4 cup crumbled fresh firm tofu
2 tbsps prepared yellow mustard
2 tbsps lemon juice
1 tbsp soy sauce and/or your favorite soup base
1 or 2 tsps garlic powder
1 tsp onion powder or 1 tbsp onion flakes
1/2 tsp liquid smoke (optional)

Chop or grind nuts or seeds with the tomato sauce in a blender or chopper until as smooth as possible. Raw nut butter or seed meal can be used instead. Whip the tofu with the other ingredients until smooth. Combine the two mixtures. An endless variety of seasonings and flavor combinations may be added at this time, e.g. barbecue sauce, Italian herbs, pimientos, chili powder, green chilis, Greek olives, sun dried tomatoes, etc. Cook in the microwave on medium high for twenty minutes, stirring occasionally. Continue to cook in small increments until thick enough to make a good spread (or it can be cooked in a double boiler for several hours). Chilling overnight enhances the flavor. Soy whiz will keep two weeks at least in the refrigerator. It also freezes well, either by itself or in other dishes. It is good for sandwiches and hors d'oeuvres or for topping tacos, burritos, baked potatoes, crepes, pizza or polenta. It's also good tossed with pastas, as an ingredient in casseroles or in any dish that usually calls for a soft flavorful cheese.

GOOD STUFF
LOAF OR STUFFING

good

This stuffing is one of the things I like to keep handy in the freezer. I chose this name because, I always forget how good it is until I eat it. Then I find myself saying "Good Stuff".

Note: Consider all measurements approximate. This recipe is not sensitive to slight variations.

1/2 cup wild rice
1/2 cup brown rice
1 2/3 cup water or vegetable broth
3/4 cup walnuts
1/2 cup crumbled firm fresh tofu
1/2 onion
1/4 green pepper
Celery or carrots (may be optional)
1 tbsp lemon juice

2 tbsps soy sauce or dry onion soup mix
Salt, pepper, garlic, onion powder as desired
3 tbsp potato flour
Cook rice in broth or water until brown rice is done but not mushy and wild rice is still firm. Keep warm for a later process.

Finely chop walnuts, onion and green pepper and other vegetables together in blender or food processor. Combine in a bowl with warm cooked rice. Whip tofu, lemon juice, herbs and seasonings together in the blender. Add to mixture. Knead potato flour into mixture with hands until it will hold its shape. Potato flour is the bonding agent. This will not work unless mixture is warm. Use more or less potato flour to control firmness. Use to stuff buns, (see recipe pg 48) peppers, and cabbage rolls, (see recipes) or pack into a loaf pan and bake until firm and slightly brown, about 30 to 45 minutes at 350º. Serve with <u>tomato</u> sauce or gravy. *catsup*

CABBAGE ROLLS

1 head of cabbage
hot water
1 recipe of Good Stuff (see recipe page 36)
1 can tomato sauce

Cut part of the core out of the head of cabbage and put it in a large kettle. Cover with hot water. Boil for 2 or 3 minutes until leaves are limp. Cool in cold water. Peel off the leaves carefully. Trim the thickest stems flat so they will be more flexible. Place a spoonful or two of Good Stuff in each leaf, depending on the size. The smallest leaves can be combined to make a roll. Fold the side edges over. Roll up and place seam side down in a baking dish. Pour tomato sauce over the top. Cover with a lid or foil and bake at 350º for 35 minutes.

STUFFED PEPPERS

3 or 4 green peppers
1 recipe Good Stuff
1 can tomato Sauce

Cut the peppers in half lengthwise. Trim out stem, seeds and white membranes. Scald the pepper halves for 1 minute in boiling water.

Place them in a flat pan and fill them generously with Good Stuff. Put about 1/4 inch of hot water in the bottom of the dish. Bake for 45 minutes at 350º. Serve with tomato sauce.

VEGAN LOW FAT PESTO

Pesto is traditionally made with a cup of olive oil, blended with fresh basil leaves and several cloves of garlic. Sometimes pine nuts or walnuts and grated cheeses are blended in. This is served cold over hot pasta. My version has the basil, garlic and nuts with just a little olive oil for flavor, as well as whipped tofu instead of cheese.

Put the following ingredients in a blender or chopper:
1 cup fresh basil leaves (packed)
1/2 cup vegetable juice or water
1 cup of firm fresh crumbled tofu
1/3 cup walnuts or pine nuts
Lots and lots of garlic
1 to 3 tbsps olive oil (optional)
Salt to taste

Blend until ingredients are well chopped and blended into a paste. Add salt if desired. Serve over freshly cooked pasta. Makes six generous servings. If you're planning to freeze it, you may want to leave out the oil until you are ready to use it. Thaw carefully. Use low temperature if you use a microwave. Do not cook.

MARINARA SAUCE

There are a lot of good vegan recipes for marinara sauce. Nevertheless, I thought I'd tell you how I make it, in case you don't have a favorite. I like to freeze it and have it on hand. I've served it to many meat eaters, tofu haters and even children and they all gobbled it up.

The amount and kind of seasonings are left open. Taste and try until you're satisfied.
2 tbsps olive oil (optional)
2 medium onions - chopped
1 medium carrot - finely chopped

1/2 green pepper - chopped
Fresh or powdered garlic
1 cup crumbled tofu
Chopped parsley
4 cups tomato sauce (4 8 0z cans)
1 1/2 cups vegetable broth (optional)
Dried basil, oregano, or mixed Italian spices

Optional: fennel seeds, rosemary, a little wine or a touch of soy sauce, soup base, or whole bay leaves (remove before serving).
Sauté onions, carrot and green pepper, with or without the olive oil until translucent and slightly brown. Add garlic, parsley, crumbled tofu and basic spices. Stir and cook a minute more. Pour in tomato sauce, broth and optional spices. Simmer for fifteen minutes or more, tasting and adding spices if desired. I freeze individual and company size portions in plastic bags.

VARIATION: PASTA PRIMAVERA: This recipe reduces the calorie content of spaghetti by replacing some of the pasta with low calorie vegetables.

Coarsely chop your choice of mushrooms, zucchini squash, spinach, broccoli, asparagus or other vegetables. Sauté with the onions in the first step.

SUPER QUICK MARINARA SAUCE

The quickest way to a fairly good marinara sauce is to take a commercially-made brand and play with it. No matter how good it is when it goes in the jar, remember, freshly added herbs at the end perk up any food.

Heat 1 jar of marinara sauce, add 1/2 cup crumbled tofu and any or all of the following seasonings: garlic, basil, oregano, mixed Italian spices, a splash of dry wine or other favorites. Simmer briefly and use on spaghetti or in other Italian recipes.

LASAGNA

8 oz package lasagna noodles
2 or 3 cups marinara sauce
2/3 cup soy whiz (see recipe, page 25)
1 onion - chopped
Your choice of any or all of the following: spinach, eggplant, mush-

rooms, zucchini or green peppers.

Cook noodles in boiling salted water. Non-stick spray will help prevent noodles from boiling over and help keep them separated. While noodles are cooking, prepare the vegetables. Eggplant should be sliced and grilled slightly in a non-stick skillet. Spinach should be steamed enough to wilt. Other vegetables should be chopped or sliced. Prepare a non-stick baking dish. Start with a thin layer of sauce. Lay out noodles to cover the bottom of the dish, dot with part of the soy whiz. Add layers of vegetables, topping with more sauce. Repeat layering, ending with noodles on top. Add a little more soy whiz and top generously with sauce. Bake in 350º oven for 45 minutes. Let stand a few minutes. Cut in squares and serve.

GOURMET TWO SAUCE LASAGNA

I have observed that famous chefs on cooking shows use an inner cream sauce and an outer marinara sauce when making lasagna. I tried my own version and it turned out quite well!

Prepare one recipe of non-fat or low-fat white sauce. Follow the previous lasagna recipe with one exception. Use the marinara sauce under the bottom layer and over the top layer. Use the white sauce in between the inner layers.

MANICOTTI FLORENTINE

This is a little elaborate, but makes a good dish for special guests.

8 large manicotti
6 to 8 cups water
1 tsp salt
2 recipes of tofu ricotta (see recipe page 34)
1 10 oz pkg frozen or 1 bunch fresh chopped spinach
1 tsp garlic powder, or minced garlic
2 tsps onion powder
3 cups marinara sauce
1/4 cup soy whiz (see recipe page 35)

Cook the manicotti in boiling salted water for about 8 minutes. They should still be firm enough to hold their shape. Thaw and drain the frozen spinach. For fresh spinach, wash well, chop, and then steam just enough to wilt. Drain well. Mix with ricotta, garlic and onion. Select a flat baking dish just big enough to hold the manicotti. Put 1 1/2 cups marinara sauce in the bottom. Stuff the manicotti using a teaspoon and place in the dish. If any have split, fill and place split side down.

Pour the remaining marinara sauce on top. Cover with a lid or foil. Bake about 40 minutes at 350º. Dot with the soy whiz and return to the oven for a few minutes. Makes 4 servings.

VARIATIONS: Use other greens or finely chopped squash or eggplant instead of spinach.

PASTA WITH GREEK OLIVES AND SUN DRIED TOMATOES

This is more of a method than a recipe. Great tasting pasta dishes can be made from whatever is in season. This dish may be a welcome change from the traditional marinara sauce. It is essentially a combination of sautéed pungent seasonings and fresh vegetables. Then the cooked pasta is added and sautéed in the same pan. Gourmet restaurants serve many similar dishes, but most depend on cheese and lots of oil. The amounts in this recipe are only suggestions. Feel free to play with this one.

1/2 lb spaghetti (whole wheat, artichoke or whatever)
6 cups water
1/2 tsp salt (optional)
12 sundried tomato halves
2/3 cup hot water
1/2 cup chopped Greek olives
3 strips of veggie bacon chopped (optional)
1 chopped onion
1/4 cup chopped parsley
1/2 cup each of 2 or more chopped vegetables e.g. zucchini, green or red sweet peppers, broccoli, fresh greens etc.
4 cloves fresh garlic or 1 1/2 tsp garlic powder
1 tsp crumbled dried oregano leaves
1 tsp crumbled dried basil leaves
dried rosemary and/or other mixed Italian spices to taste
1/4 cup burgundy wine (optional)
1/2 cup crumbled tofu or soy whiz
3 tbsps olive oil

Cut the Greek olives off the pits in small pieces, and set aside. Cut the sundried tomatoes in slivers with a pair of scissors. Pour hot water over them and let stand. Start the water for the pasta as you prepare the onion, parsley and other vegetables. Put the pasta on to cook.

If you choose the veggie bacon, cook it first in a large non-stick skillet. When it's crisp, add the onions, parsley and other veggies. Sauté (fat-free of course). When partially cooked, sprinkle in the spices and garlic. (Slight toasting improves the flavor of herbs). Add the wine and a tablespoon or two of water as needed and saute` until the onions are translucent. Stir in the Greek olives, the sundried tomatoes (water and all) and the tofu or soy whiz.

When the pasta is done, drain it well and add it to the mixture in the skillet. Drizzle the olive oil over the pasta. Toss and cook for several minutes. It's done when the pasta is coated with the oil and seasonings and is almost chewy. Makes 3 or 4 servings.

SUMMER SPAGHETTI

I call this dish Summer Spaghetti for two reasons: it's best made with freshly picked summer tomatoes and garden herbs. It requires only a minimum amount of cooking on a hot summer day.

1/2 lb spaghetti
6 cups water
1/2 tsp salt
2 tbsps olive oil
2 to 4 cloves garlic
1/2 tsp dried oregano (optional)
1/4 cup tofu ricotta (see recipe page 34)
1 cup diced tomatoes
2 or 3 green onions - chopped
2 tbsps fresh basil - chopped, (or other fresh herbs)

Bring the water to a boil, add salt and the spaghetti. Put the garlic through a press and combine with the olive oil. Chop the tomatoes, green onions and herbs. When the spaghetti is done, drain well. Put the pan back onto the warm burner and add the olive oil, garlic, and oregano. Toss with the pasta. Next add the tofu ricotta and toss until evenly coated. Put on a serving dish or individual plates and top with the chopped tomatoes, basil and green onions. Makes 3 or 4 servings.

BAKED POLENTA

Polenta is a traditional dish that took Italian grandmothers hours of cooking and stirring to prepare. I cook it in the microwave. It's a lot easier.

1 cup polenta (coarse corn meal)
3 1/2 cups water
1/2 tsp salt (optional)

Put meal and water (and salt) in a 2 quart bowl. Microwave for 10 minutes on high. Stir. Cook on medium heat 6 to 8 minutes, or until mush is thick and well cooked. Spread in a baking pan like a crust, about 1/2 inch thick. Use the back of a spoon moistened in cold water to spread smoothly. Bake in a 350º oven for 1/2 hour. Refrigerate or freeze for later use or fill with one of the following:

Italian style - Top pizza style with a layer of soy whiz and/or chopped vegetables. Add a layer of marinara sauce and bake another 1/2 hour. Let stand a few minutes to set. Slice and serve.

Mexican style - Top polenta with layers of soy whiz and refried beans. Bake 1/2 hour. Serve with salsa and/or chopped tomatoes, green onions and avocados.

Hors d'oeuvres - Make a thinner polenta crust (about 1/4 inch), bake longer until quite crusty and brown. Cover with soy whiz alone or with beans and/or sauce. Bake another 15 minutes. Cool and cut into bite-sized squares. It should be firm enough to pick up with your fingers.

POTATO CAKES OR KUGEL

1 cup shredded raw potatoes (about 1 large potato)
1/4 cup finely chopped onions
1/2 cup tofu ricotta (see recipe page 34)
2 tsps lemon juice
1/4 tsp salt (optional)
Pepper (optional)
1/2 tsp garlic powder (optional)

Add the lemon juice, salt, pepper and garlic powder to the ricotta. Set aside 1/2 of the ricotta mix. Put the rest in a bowl with the shredded potatoes and onions. Mix thoroughly (hands work best). Preheat a large iron non-stick sprayed skillet to medium high. Put the mixture in the skillet as four small cakes or one large one. Pat down with a spatula to make them firm and flat. Turn the burner down to medium, cover and cook until brown (about 5 minutes). Turn, cover and brown well on the other side. Add a tablespoon or two of water to the pan and cover. Cook until the water has cooked off. Repeat this procedure until the cakes are done all the way through. Uncover and let brown a little more. Top with remaining seasoned tofu ricotta and serve. Variations: Start with pre-cooked shredded potatoes. It's faster, but I just happen to prefer to start with them raw.

For Kugel - Double the recipe. Pack down in a flat non-stick sprayed baking dish. The mixture should be about 1/2 to 3/4 inch deep. Spray the top for better browning. Bake at 350º for 30 minutes. Remove and spread remaining tofu ricotta on top (soy whiz is good for this too). Return to oven for 10 minutes. Let cool slightly to set. Cut in squares. This can be chilled and cut into bite-sized squares for hors d'oeuvres.

TACOS, TOSTADAS AND BURRITOS

I've grouped these three recipes together because they are just slight variations of the same ingredients. A good way to serve them to family and friends is to put everything on the table in bowls and encourage people to build their own. The tortillas will stay warm if put on a warm plate and covered with a cloth or paper towel.

FOR TACOS - Have ready the following:
Refried Beans - Freshly cooked beans are nice, but there are good, lard free, canned ones, as well as dry bean flakes, plain or seasoned. The flakes are very convenient, especially for just one or two servings.

Salsa or taco sauce - either fresh or bottled; mild or hot, as you like
Cooked Brown Rice - (optional)
Shredded Cabbage and/or lettuce. (In parts of Mexico cabbage is the favorite. You might want to try it.)
Tomatoes and green onions - chopped.
Sliced olives or hot peppers (optional)
Soy Whiz (see recipe page 35)
Tofu Ricotta (optional) (see recipe page 34)
Corn Tortillas

Heat the beans (and rice). If the beans are unseasoned, stir in a tablespoon or two of salsa or taco sauce. Heat the tortillas on a grill or in the oven, until slightly dried out, but still very flexible. Spoon a line of beans in the middle of the tortilla. Add rice if desired, soy whiz, salsa and shredded cabbage or lettuce, and top with chopped tomatoes and green onions, etc. Fold over and eat.

FOR TOSTADAS - For most part, these are a different arrangement of the ingredients in tacos, with more emphasis on the raw vegetables. In effect it's more of a Mexican salad. The only added ingredient is salad dressing.

Heat the tortillas on a grill or in the oven until a little crisp. Place a tortilla on a plate. Top with layers of beans, rice, salsa, and dabs of soy whiz. Heap with a salad made with shredded cabbage, salad greens, or other raw vegetables. Garnish with tomato wedges, green onions, tofu ricotta (optional) and top with your favorite salad dressing.

FOR BURRITOS - These are made with large flour tortillas, and are similar to tacos, with more emphasis on the beans and rice and less on the chopped vegetables. Put a generous line of the beans and rice in the middle of the tortilla, along with your choice of salsa, soy whiz, and/or tofu ricotta. Sprinkle with some chopped tomatoes, green onions, shredded cabbage or lettuce, sliced olives or hot peppers. Turn up the bottom and roll up from the sides. It's easier to pick up and eat, if you wrap it in a waxed paper, or you can put it on a plate and eat it with a knife and fork.

To Microwave: Put cold beans, rice, salsa and soy whiz on a tortilla. Roll up and put on a plate. Cover lightly with a paper towel and microwave on high for three minutes. Open and add ricotta and shredded vegtables.

ENCHILADAS

1 cup salsa, fresh or bottled, mild or hot
1 cup tomato sauce (8 oz can)
1 cup water
2 tbsps corn starch
Garlic and chili powder to taste
1 3/4 cups refried beans (16 oz can)
1 cup cooked brown rice
3/4 cup soy whiz (see recipe pg 35)
12 corn tortillas
3/4 cup tofu ricotta (see recipe pg 34)

In a saucepan, mix the cornstarch and water. Add the salsa, tomato sauce, garlic and chili powder and bring to a boil until slightly thickened, creating a sauce. Put a thin layer of the sauce in the bottom of a flat non-stick or treated baking dish. Warm the tortillas on a grill. Fill with beans, rice and soy whiz. Roll and place in the dish, folded side down. Top with the remaining sauce and bake for 40 minutes at 350º. Garnish with tofu ricotta, and your choice of chopped cilantro, green onions, and/or tomatoes.

PART FOUR - COOKING WITH OKARA

Okara is the fiber or mash left over after making soy milk. It is a nutritious food which is high in fiber, and in some instances can act as an egg substitute. Nutritionally, in addition to the fiber content it has even more calcium and potassium than soy milk. It also contains protein, is low in fat and is free of cholesterol and sodium.

Chapter Ten
OKARA BURGERS AND SAUSAGE

Basic mix:
For each cup of warm okara add:
1 1/2 tbsp soy sauce
2 tsps onion powder or flakes
1 tsp or more minced garlic or garlic powder
1/2 tsp liquid smoke (optional)
3 tbsps potato flour

Work the ingredients together with your hands until the mixture will hold its shape. This will not happen unless the okara is quite warm. If it's too dry, add a few drops of water to achieve desired texture. Form into patties and bake on a cookie sheet at 300º for 30 minutes. These freeze well. Serving suggestions: Brown slightly in a skillet with or without oil and serve on a bun or brown and serve with country gravy (recipe in soy milk section).

To make sausage-like patties - Add one of the following combinations of seasonings before mixing or make up your own.

Country sausage - 1/4 tsp coriander, 1/4 tsp marjoram, 1/4 tsp savory, 1/4 tsp lemon pepper and 1 tsp poultry seasoning.

Hot Italian sausage - 1 tsp powdered fennel, 1 tsp chili powder, 1/2 tsp. poultry seasoning, 1/4 tsp oregano, and 1/2 tsp black pepper.

To make sausage bits - Crumble and toast the sausage mixture in a skillet or on a cookie sheet, with or without oil, until brown and dry. Store in a jar and use in the recipes or as a garnish for salads, pizzas, etc. Use to make sausage gravy (see country gravy on page 14). Add to spaghetti sauce for flavor and added protein.

SCRAPPLE
What's Scrapple?

Many of you may have never heard of scrapple. It was one of the ways pioneers used every bit of food available to them. After making sausage, they would boil the bones, pick off the little bits of meat less thrifty people would throw away. When thickened with cornmeal and sliced and fried, it was a delicious part of an old fashioned harvest breakfast. This version is similar in nutrition and flavor with the soy and corn providing complementary protein.

1 cup polenta (coarse corn meal)
3 1/2 cups liquid (at least part vegetable broth)
1 tsp dried onions or powder
1/2 tsp salt (optional)
1/2 cup okara hot Italian sausage bits (see above)

Put cornmeal, liquid, salt, and onions in a large, deep bowl and micro-wave on high for 12 to 15 minutes until most of liquid is absorbed. Stir in sausage bits and cook on medium for an additional 5 to 10 minutes, stirring once or twice. The mush should be thick and well cooked. Turn into a loaf pan rinsed with cold water. Chill thoroughly. Unmold and slice. Brown in a skillet, with or without oil or butter. If slices are thin enough, they can be baked quite crisp in a 400º oven. Cooking time will vary according to the moisture content of the scrapple.

Wrap leftovers and refrigerate or freeze.

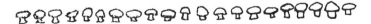

Okara allows you to make a high fiber bread that is light in color. If you don't have any okara (a by product of making soy milk) these yeast bread recipes work fine without it.

OKARA YEAST BREAD

1 tbsp active dry yeast
2/3 cup lukewarm water
2 cups hot water
1/2 cup okara (4 cubes)
2 tbsps apple juice concentrate or 1 tbsp sugar
1 tbsp vegetable oil (optional)
1 tsp salt (optional)
3 cups stone ground whole wheat flour
3 cups unbleached bread flour

Sprinkle yeast over warm water in a small bowl and set aside. Put the hot water in a large mixing bowl. Add okara, sweetener, shortening, and salt. Stir in 2 cups of the unbleached flour and beat with a wire whisk for about a minute. Add yeast mix and beat for another minute. Work in whole wheat flour and part of the remaining unbleached flour, using hands when it becomes stiff. Knead in enough of the remaining unbleached flour to make a smooth elastic dough (about 2 or 3 minutes). Use a little more flour if needed. I knead right in the bowl like my mother did. This dough will be warm to the touch and if kept slightly warm it will rise to double in size in 1/2 hour. Punch down and form into loaves or buns. Let rise again 20 or 30 minutes. Bake in 400º oven for 20 minutes for rolls or 40 minutes for loaves. To make it more crusty like french bread, place a small pan of water in the oven when you turn it on to preheat. Makes two 1 lb loaves. This dough can be used for sandwich rolls, dinner rolls, sweet rolls, french bread, etc.

STUFFED BUNS

Stuffed buns can be filled with almost anything that is thick enough to spoon onto rounds of dough without running off (chilling helps). Two of my favorites are "Soy Whiz" and "Good Stuff" (see recipes pages 35, 36). These buns freeze well and are great finger foods for picnics and traveling. At home they can be served hot with dipping sauces or gravy. You can use Chinese, Italian or Mexican filling or leftovers of any kind. Chopped fruit and nuts make good fillings too.

Prepare 1 recipe of bread dough. Let rise and punch down. Divide part of the dough into egg sized balls. Pat out on floured board until thin (about 1/4 inch). Make sure the edges are thin also. Place a spoonful of filling in the center. Stretch and pull sides of dough up and over the filling and pinch together over the top. There will be excess dough at the top. Twist and pull off the excess dough and set aside to use again. Place buns on a baking sheet, with seam side down. Before baking, prick a small hole in the top. Repeat procedure until you are out of dough or filling. Let rise 10-15 minutes. Bake at 400º, 15 to 20. minutes.

Options: These also can be steamed Chinese style.

SWEET ROLLS

My favorite sweet treat is very simple to make. Melt 1 or 2 tablespsoons of margarine in the bottom a small flat baking dish. In a separate dish, mix together one or two tablespoons of sugar or fructose and some cinnamon. Make little balls of dough, walnut size or less. Roll in margarine and then sugar mix. Put in the baking dish. Continue until it is full. Let rise and bake until brown.

This basic bread dough can be used for any type of cinnamon rolls or other pastries. If desired the dough can be enriched by adding a little extra sweetener, and oil or margarine at the beginning.

VEGAN PIZZA

There are no amounts listed in this recipe because it's up to you to wing it. Use your favorite toppings, or whatever you have on hand. Yeast dough that has risen once and your favorite marinara sauce (homemade or not) are the mandatory ingredients. Pat out yeast dough, which has risen once, in an iron skillet or large square baking dish. Make less than 1/4 inch thick for regular pizza, or thicker if you prefer deep dish. Brush with olive oil (optional). Dot on or spread on a layer of soy whiz (see recipe page 35). Cover with a generous layer of sauce. Top with your choice of any combination of the following:

Onion rings, chopped garlic, zucchini slices, green peppers, mushrooms or other vegetables.
Artichoke hearts or olives.
Soy sausage (see recipe page 46) or bacon bits, baked tofu strips or whatever else you like.

Brush the top with olive oil or a thin layer of sauce. Bake on the bottom shelf in a preheated oven at 400º for about 25 minutes.

VARIATION - If you prefer, bake on just marinara sauce, and soy whiz. Remove from the oven and add avocado, raw chopped tomatoes, green onions, basil, parsley and other herbs.

Chapter Twelve
OKARA AS AN EGG SUBSTITUTE

Okara as an egg substitute allows pancakes, waffles, muffins, and scones to be back on the menu. I like a blend of half whole wheat and unbleached flour. The okara substitutes for the extra fiber in 100% whole wheat. There are many great combinations. I hope you'll try them.

BASIC BAKING MIX

To save time, I make up a mix that can be put in a jar or canister and used as needed. It's especially nice for making single servings.

2 cups stone ground whole wheat flour
2 cups unbleached flour
4 tsps baking powder
4 tbsps corn starch
1 tsp salt (optional)
Place all of the ingredients in a large bowl. Sift, or stir with your hands, until well mixed. Store for use in recipes following.

PANCAKES OR WAFFLES

Whisk together in mixing bowl:
1/4 cup okara (2 cubes)
1 cup water
1 or 2 tbsps vegetable oil (optional for pancakes, a must for waffles.)
Add 1 cup baking mix
        -or-
Mix together dry ingredients:
1/2 cup whole wheat flour
1/2 cup unbleached flour
1 tsp baking powder
1 tbsp corn starch
1/2 tsp salt

Add dry ingredients to wet ones and beat into a nice batter. Add a little more water or flour if needed. Makes two servings.

MUFFINS OR COFFEE CAKE

Plain:
Whisk together in a mixing bowl:
1 cup water
1/4 cup (2 cubes) okara
1/3 to 2/3 cup sugar or fructose to taste (see sweetening alternatives)
2 tbsps vegetable oil (optional)
Vanilla to taste

Add 2 cups baking mix
          -or-
1 cup whole wheat flour
1 cup unbleached flour
2 tsps baking powder
2 tbsps corn starch.
1/2 tsp salt

Stir dry ingredients to mix. Add to wet ingredients and stir in very gently until just wet. Do not beat. Spoon into non stick treated muffin cups or into 8 or 9 inch square baking dish. Cook at 350º for 25 to 35 minutes.

I seldom make plain muffins. Any number of fruit, nut, or spice combinations can be added to muffins. Here are some of my favorites:

Almond poppy seed - Add to wet ingredients, 1 tsp. almond extract, 1 tbsp poppy seeds and 1/4 cup chopped almonds.

Gingerbread - Sweeten with 1/2 cup molasses and add 2 tsp ground ginger to the dry ingredients.

Raisin walnut - Add to dry ingredients, 1/3 cup raisins, 1/3 cup walnuts, 1/2 tsp cinnamon, 1/2 tsp pumpkin pie spice.

Lemon - Add to wet ingredients, 1/2 cup lemon juice, freshly grated lemon peel or 1 tsp dried lemon peel, 1 tsp. lemon extract and 1/4 cup more sweetener.

Anise seed - Add to basic recipe, 1 tbsp anise seed.

For biscotti - Make an anise coffee cake. Take out of the oven when it is done, leaving the oven on. Partially cool (about ten minutes), slice and lay on a cookie sheet. Put back in the oven and turn the oven off. Leave in until oven is cold (several hours). The biscotti should be dry and hard. If it's still moist, reheat a little and turn oven off again. If biscotti is thoroughly dry, it will keep almost indefinitely at room temperature. This is a delicious munchie and can be dunked if it's too hard to chew.

LOW FAT BISCUITS, SCONES OR CRUST

Biscuits and pie crust taste awfully good, but they are very high in fat and have no place in a healthy diet. I don't claim my version tastes the same, but it does have a fresh hot bread quality that makes it very tasty, especially with country sausage gravy (see soy milk section page 15).

For biscuits - Make 1 recipe of muffins, omitting sweetener and vanilla. Reduce the water to 3/4 cup. Drop by spoonfuls on a cookie sheet. Pat gently into more biscuit like shape if desired. It's important not to over handle the dough. Bake at 400º for 25 minutes or until brown.

For making pot pie - Prepare your favorite vegan stew or other filling and put in a flat baking dish. Pat out biscuit dough to appropriate shape, lay gently on top of filling and bake at 350º until filling is cooked and crust is brown. This will work as dumplings as well.

For cobbler - Fill a flat dish with your favorite fruit pie filling. It tastes good to slightly sweeten crust and add vanilla.

For scones - Use cobbler topping recipe but cook like biscuits. Brush tops with soy milk and sprinkle a little sugar on top.

PART FIVE - MAKING IT WORK

Chapter Thirteen
THE DANCE

I love to cook, and I enjoy experiencing a cooking frenzy I call "The Dance." It may seem a little complicated at first, but after a few times it weaves together, very much as though it was choreographed. While one thing is cooking or cooling, I'm doing another, or making preparations for the next step. While I'm in the kitchen anyway, if I stay focused, I can accomplish enough to reduce my future time in the kitchen by many hours. On a practical note, I buy my tofu unless it is unavailable for some reason. However, the home made soy milk is a big saving of money (it's good too), and okara can only be obtained by making it.

Your rhythm may be different from mine but this is what works for me. As much as I love to cook, when I'm having a busy day and I'm immersed in another project. I'm always glad I did the dance in advance!

HOW DOES THE DANCE GO? The soybeans have to be soaked all night. I start in the morning with the pre-soaked soybeans and make the soy milk (see recipe), which creates okara (soy fiber) as a by-product.

If I decide I'm going to make tofu out of all, or part of the soy milk, I do that next, setting the okara aside.

When the tofu is made and setting up in the mold, I use some of the okara to start a batch of yeast bread (see recipe page 48). This is a very thrifty thing to do, and the bread is delicious and wholesome. My bread recipe is fast and will be completed within two hours.

If you don't want to make the bread, use this time to make a batch of Basic Baking Mix (see recipe page 50), that can be used with okara for eggless pancakes, muffins, etc. For a big family make a double batch of the mix. It will fit nicely into a gallon container. You may want to make some muffins at this time.

While the dough is rising (about 1/2 hour), I make part of the okara into burgers, sausage patties or bits and cook them according

to instructions. I reserve some okara to use in baking in the coming week and freeze the rest in ice cube trays.

I punch down the bread dough and form it into buns, loaves or sweet rolls. If I have prepared a filling in advance or have some in the freezer, I can make stuffed buns with part of the dough and make a loaf with the rest.

While the bread is rising again, I have time to get the tofu finished and in the refrigerator along with the soy milk. If I have enough ice cube trays and room in the freezer, I'll freeze part of the milk at this time, saving the rest to use fresh for soups, casseroles and sauces. By now, the burgers should be ready to freeze as well.

While the bread is baking, tofu can be used to make Soy Whiz or Tofu Ricotta. White sauce or milk gravy can be made from part of the soy milk. All of these recipes freeze well.

I usually find time to clean up as I go and then prepare for the next step.

By lunch time, I can sit down to a nice burger with pickles, mustard and tomatoes on a homemade sandwich roll. I may make one of the quick soups in a bowl to fill out the menu. If I choose to, I can finish my meal with a freshly baked sweet roll. The dance is complete when I store or freeze all the things I've prepared and I walk away with a tremendous sense of satisfaction.

Chapter Fourteen
WHAT'S ON THE MENU

Our family had a wonderful feast last Thanksgiving. We started out with RAW VEGGIES AND CHIPS with ONION FLAVORED SOY WHIZ DIP. For the first time we had as many vegans as meat eaters. We did a small traditional TURKEY with DRESSING and GRAVY for those who wanted it.

For the vegans, we had BAKED TOFU, a large casserole of GOOD STUFF and VEGAN GRAVY. We all shared the MASHED POTATOES, SALADS, ROASTED SWEET POTATOES WITH PECANS and OKARA DINNER ROLLS. A guest brought BAKED TOMATO HALVES topped with seasoned bread crumbs. For dessert we had the choice of PUMPKIN or FRUIT PIES. Everyone considered it a worthy holiday repast.

WHAT'S FOR DINNER

1. PASTA with PESTO or MARINARA SAUCE, fresh made GARLIC BREAD or BREAD STICKS. Steamed BROCCOLI, ASPARAGUS or other seasonal veggies, GREEN SALAD with LOW-FAT FRENCH DRESSING
2. MANICOTTI FLORENTINE, green salad, with LOW-FAT GREEK OLIVE & SUN DRIED TOMATO DRESSING
3. ROASTED VEGETABLES and TOFU, shredded cabbage with LOW-FAT HONEY DIJON DRESSING
4. QUICK CHINESE SOUP, BRAISED TOFU WITH STIR-FRY VEG- ETABLES and TOFU FRIED RICE
5. Spinach, artichoke or other dinner CREPES. For dessert, serve CREPES filled with fresh fruit and sweetened TOFU RICOTTA
6. SUMMER SPAGHETTI, steamed vegetables and fresh fruit salad with LOW-FAT HONEY DIJON DRESSING
7. STUFFED PEPPERS, SCALLOPED POTATOES and a green salad with LOW-FAT FRENCH DRESSING
8. FAJITAS, corn chips and green salad with LOW-FAT FRENCH DRESSING
9. COUNTRY SAUSAGE GRAVY, mashed potatoes, and fresh sliced tomatoes, cucumbers and other raw vegetables.

FOR POT LUCKS AND PICNICS

1. BARBECUED TOFU KABOBS
2. CHINESE TOFU SALAD WITH PEANUT SAUCE
3. Fresh fruit salad with TOFU RICOTTA and LOW-FAT HONEY DIJON DRESSING
4. STUFFED BUNS
5. GARLIC BREAD (homemade of course)
6. Bite sized POLENTA SQUARES
7. Chili flavored SOY WHIZ DIP with corn chips
8. Onion flavored SOY WHIZ DIP with veggies
9. Chocolate PIE topped with ORANGE TOFU SPREAD
10. PUMPKIN PIE
11. TAPIOCA PUDDING with fresh peaches
12. SOY NUTS

FOR LUNCH

1. Any of the soups with OKARA BREAD, such as QUICK CREAM SOUP, OLD FASHIONED TOMATO SOUP, QUICK CHINESE SOUP, OR JEWISH CABBAGE SOUP

2. OKARA BURGERS or SAUSAGE on a bun with all the trimmings and ROASTED POTATO SLICES on the side
3. BAKED TOFU sandwich, with mustard, dill pickles and ketchup.
4. A bean and/or rice BURRITO made with SOY WHIZ, lettuce, tomatoes, and salsa, rolled up in a whole wheat tortilla
5. A tostada made with a corn tortilla, refried beans, SOY WHIZ, and salsa, covered with shredded lettuce, tomato slices and topped with LOW-FAT FRENCH DRESSING
6. Sandwiches made with Greek olive and sun dried tomato flavored SOY WHIZ.

FOR BREAKFAST

1. Cereal with SOY AND RICE MILK BLEND, powdered vanilla, sweetener and chopped nuts
2. MUFFINS or COFFEE CAKE
3. Scrambled TOFU and toasted OKARA BREAD
4. POTATO CAKES
5. OKARA PANCAKES with applesauce and cinnamon
6. LOW FAT BISCUITS with COUNTRY SAUSAGE GRAVY
7. SCONES with fruit only jam
8. BANANA NOG
9. For a special breakfast or dessert, serve an OKARA WAFFLE with fresh strawberries or peaches, topped with sweetened TOFU RICOTTA or ORANGE TOFU SPREAD

Chapter Fifteen
THE LAST ROUND UP

There are a few more recipes I just couldn't leave out. Some don't contain soy products, but are useful in adding a finishing touch, or a little extra flavor to a meal.

VEGETABLE BROTH - There is a fairly good canned vegetable broth on the market, but if it's homemade, you know what's in it. Vegetable broth is used for any recipe that would traditionally call for beef or poultry stock. This basic ingredient is handy to have in the freezer in cubes or small tubs. It's quite concentrated and in addition to soups, it will add flavor to pasta sauces, vegetable stews, gravies and more. It can be made salt free, to be seasoned when used. This broth is loaded with potassium and other good things.

BASIC VEGETABLE BROTH

3 or 4 large onions peeled and quartered
4 or 5 celery stalks and leaves - halved
2 or 3 carrots - in chunks
3 or 4 cloves garlic peeled
2 medium potatoes, in chunks
1/2 bunch parsley
squash, string beans, chard or other vegetables in season (optional)
salt (optional)

Place all of the vegetables in a large pot and cover with water. Bring to a boil and reduce heat. Cover and simmer for 3 hours. Strain off broth and throw vegetables away. The broth will be quite concentrated. If you want it even more so, simmer awhile with the lid off to reduce the volume.

For a little different flavor, start out as above but add 1 or 2 cups of dry wine, mushrooms and/or some herbs, such as bay leaves, peppercorns, thyme or your own favorites.

GRAVY

Good gravy has always been an important part of cooking. It has always been thought of as fattening, because it is made from greasy meat drippings. Now we know we can have flavorful gravy without the fat.

In the soy milk section there are several recipes for milk gravy. Most other gravies are, in essence, thickened broth. A well-flavored broth, makes a well-flavored gravy. Always taste and adjust.

Some people prefer cornstarch for thickening and others prefer flour. I'll give you recipes for both. All of the gravies are fat free. A lot of gravy mixes are available in the stores and soup mixes can be thickened to make gravy as well. However, that's a lot to pay for something that is so simple to make yourself. If you want to use them, it's important to read labels to see if they contain things you don't want.

All of these methods may be used to thicken vegetable stews, pot pie fillings and casseroles.

SIMPLE GRAVY NO. 1 - Make a broth of 1 CUP WATER, 2 TBSPS SOY SAUCE, (OR 2 TSP MISO) 2 TSPS MINCED GARLIC AND 1/2 TSP MINCED GINGER. Put in a sauce pan on medium heat. Mix together 1/4 CUP COLD WATER and 2 TBSPS CORN STARCH. Stir into hot broth and bring to a boil until it thickens.

SIMPLE GRAVY NO. 2 - Put 1 CUP VEGETABLE BROTH, 1 TBSP. SOY SAUCE or 1 TSP MISO, 1 TSP KITCHEN BOUQUET, and 1 TSP GARLIC POWDER, in a sauce pan, over medium heat. Mix 1/2 CUP COLD WATER and 3 TBSPS FLOUR in the blender. Stir into the hot liquid, and bring to a boil until it thickens.

SIMPLE GRAVY NO. 3 - Heat the broth of your choice to a simmer. Sprinkle in Wondra Flour, a little at a time, until it reaches the desired thickness.

DELUXE GRAVY - Mix I CUP OF FLAVORFUL BROTH. Set aside. Sauté some finely chopped onions and/or mushrooms until translucent. Add the broth and perhaps a BAY LEAF, some pepper, and maybe a little WINE. Toast 1/4 CUP FLOUR in a dry skillet until brown. Blend with 3/4 CUP COLD WATER in the blender. Stir most of the mixture into the hot broth. Bring it to a boil and check for thickness. Add more thickening or water as needed.

VEGAN STEW - Start out as you would for DELUXE GRAVY. If you want to, you may brown SEITAN CUBES (WHEAT GLUTEN) or BAKED TOFU PIECES with the ONIONS AND MUSHROOMS. When you add the BROTH, BAY LEAF and WINE, put in POTATOES, CARROTS, PARSLEY, CELERY and OTHER VEGGIES and cook until done. Thicken with browned flour and water as in the gravy recipe.

SOY NUTS

These make a good snack and keep without refrigeration. They are available in stores, but they're better tasting made fresh and they certainly cost less.

1/2 lb soy beans (1 1/2 cups)
3 cups cold water
1/2 tsp salt (optional)

Rinse the soy beans and put in a saucepan with the water and salt. Bring to a full rolling boil. Remove from the heat a and let soak 2 hours. Drain well. Spread out on a cookie sheet one layer deep. Pick out any broken pieces. Do not crowd. Bake in a preheated 350º oven until brown and crisp. Time will vary from 45 minutes to an hour or more. I like mine extra crisp.

VARIATIONS: Mix 2 tablespoons soy or teriyaki sauce with garlic, onion powder or liquid smoke and toss with the drained beans. Bake as above.

SOY COFFEE

This is surprisingly good. Perhaps because it is a bean, the taste resembles coffee in a different way than beverages made from roasted grains. Even served black, it is quite tasty, and it lends itself well to vegan cafe` au lait with milk,vanilla and spices etc. (see recipes page 26).

It's made like soy nuts without the salt. Bake them longer until they're as dark brown as coffee. Turn off the oven and let them brown even more as they cool.

To prepare, grind fine in a coffee grinder. It grinds differently than regular coffee and tends to clog up filters. Two ways of preparation work best. You can use a stove top percolator or make it like "old fashioned cowboy coffee," where you just boil it with water, let it stand to settle and pour off the top. It can be mixed with regular coffee if you'd like.

QUICK SOUPS IN A BOWL

A bowl of freshly made soup and some good bread tastes great on a winter day. Two of the fastest soups are the QUICK CREAM SOUP and OLD FASHIONED TOMATO SOUP in the soy milk section. Here are a few more soups, made in the bowl in the microwave for one or two quick servings.

FOR VEGETABLE SOUP: Put a cup of V8 vegetable juice, VEGETABLE BROTH or boullion in a bowl. Add a small amount of your choice of the following: chopped FRESH or DRIED ONIONS, CELERY, PARSLEY, CARROTS, POTATOES or other vegetables you have handy. Cook in the microwave on high for 5 minutes. Check for doneness and flavor. Crumble in some tofu, add garlic powder or other seasonings if needed and cook until done.

JEWISH CABBAGE SOUP: For each serving, put in a bowl, 1 CUP CANNED DICED TOMATOES, 1 CUP WATER, 1 CUP FINELY SHREDDED CABBAGE, 1 TBSP LEMON JUICE or CIDER VINEGAR and 1 TBSP SUGAR OR HONEY. Cook in the microwave 7 or 8 minutes until cabbage is tender. Top with a dollop of TOFU RICOTTA (see recipe page 34).

QUICK CHINESE SOUP: Put 2 1/2 CUPS WATER and 1 1/2 TBSPS SOY OR TERIYAKI SAUCE in a large bowl. Add chopped GREEN ONIONS, CELERY, a RADISH, PARSLEY and a few FROZEN PEAS. Cook on high for 3 minutes. Add some crumbled RAMEN NOODLES and some DICED TOFU. Cook 2 more minutes. Let stand a minute. Add a few drops of SESAME OIL and serve.

LOW-FAT SALAD DRESSINGS

Here are some recipes for low-fat salad dressings. If mixed with whipped tofu, they can be turned into creamy dressings, dips or baked potato toppings.

LOW-FAT FRENCH DRESSING

1 can tomato sauce
1 tbsp olive oil
1 tsp dry mustard
1 tsp Worcestershire sauce
1 tsp garlic powder
1/2 tsp salt
1/4 tsp black pepper
Blend together and store in a jar in the refrigerator.

LOW-FAT HONEY DIJON DRESSING

This dressing is especially good on fruit salads or pasta and bean salads.

1/4 tsp powdered agar-agar
1/2 cup water
2 tbsps olive oil
1/2 cup honey
1/4 cup balsamic vinegar
3 tbsps dijon mustard
1/2 tsp salt
1 cup cold water

Boil the agar-agar in 1/2 cup water for 5 minutes. Add 1 cup of cold water and all of the other ingredients and blend thoroughly. You can substitute 1 tbsp plain Kosher gelatin for the agar-agar. Follow the package directions.

SUN DRIED TOMATO AND GREEK OLIVE DRESSING

This dressing is full flavored enough to top strong salad greens or vegetables.

12 sun dried tomato halves
1/2 cup hot water
1/4 tsp powdered agar-agar
1 1/2 cups water
1/4 cup balsamic vinegar
2 tsps garlic powder
1 tsp onion powder
2 tbsps olive oil
1/3 cup chopped Greek olives
2 tbsps honey or sugar
2 tsps dried basil leaves
I tsp oregano leaves
1/2 tsp salt

Chop sundried tomatoes with scissors. Cover with the 1/2 cup hot water and let stand. Boil the agar-agar and 1/2 cup water together for 5 minutes. Add the rest of the ingredients, letting the sundried tomatoes soak until the last. Put in the blender and blend thoroughly. Put in a jar and chill. You can substitute 1 tbsp plain Kosher gelatin for the agar-agar. Follow the package directions.

TIPS FOR NEW COOKS

This is essentially, a letter to Guy, a highly intelligent young man, who proofread this book manuscript with exquisite care. As a non-cook, he raised some questions he felt needed to be answered before he would dare try to actually cook anything! I've decided to include these suggestions, on the chance that they might be of interest to other beginning cooks.

1. It's really important when making a dish for the first time, to make sure you have all of the ingredients on hand. Follow the recipe as written. This is not the time to substitute. I have tried to give accurate amounts where it's important and give leeway where it isn't. Optional ingredients are just that. The dish can be made without them.

2. If you are the cautious type you may feel intimidated when I suggest that you experiment. That's why I usually make a specific list of ingredients to try. Be brave and put one of them in and then taste it. See if it improves the flavor, in your opinion. Take a deep breath and try more ingredients. Observe the taste after each addition. Every ingredient in a dish should contribute something, or it has no business being there! You'll begin to observe the flavor of previously unfamiliar ingredients, and in time you'll actually have the courage to try your new favorite flavors in other dishes. You might also observe any flavors you can't stand, and avoid them in the future!

3. Start with a simple recipe, with just a few ingredients, and clear directions, e.g., Quick Corn Chowder, Old Fashioned Tomato Soup, or Orange Tofu Spread.

4. Don't try out a new recipe when company's coming. Practice it in advance.

5. If you're a person who would like to throw things in with wild abandon, and create great culinary delights, take it easy at first, unless you want to waste a lot of food. That ability comes only with time. Stick to the suggested options until you learn the basic skills. If you're really interested, and willing to try, you may be surprised at how quickly you will learn.

6. Don't panic if you don't quite understand the terminology in a recipe. It will just freeze your brain and you'll be unable to use your common sense. Look calmly at the words surrounding the unfamiliar one, and notice the context in which it is used. If you still can't figure it out, call Mom! If Mom is a lousy cook, everybody has an old aunt, or a friend, or a colleague who might know the answer. If that fails, remem-

ber we're in the information age. You have available, computer dictionaries, encyclopedias, cook books, and chat rooms.

What do you do when your food isn't turning out right? It would take a whole other book to address this subject, but I'll try to give you a few practical tips.

1. Don't use one failure as an excuse to quit!

2. If it's too thick, add some of whatever liquid is used in the recipe, such as milk, water, or broth.

3. If it's too soupy, one way is to add more of the thickener used in the recipe, such as cornstarch, flour, etc. Try adding it a little at a time until it suits you. Another way to reduce the liquid in a dish is to boil it with the lid off, providing it's a dish that can stand the extra cooking. If that fails, just call it soup!

4. If it's over-seasoned, think of a way to dilute the flavor with cooked rice, potatoes or pasta. Many a new favorite casserole has been invented that way.

5. There's a time to just throw it out! It happens to the best of us. When you know you're not ever going to eat that mess, ask yourself this question. Is it more noble to let it rot in the refrigerator before throwing it out, or to have the courage to do it in the first place?

6. Anything new can be a comedy of errors at first, but remember the word comedy and don't take yourself too seriously. In a short time it really can become fun!

Love and Good Luck

Bobbi Parker

Favorites

Recipe   Pg

_____
_____
_____
_____
_____
_____
_____
_____
_____
_____
_____
_____
_____
_____
_____
_____
_____
_____
_____
_____
_____
_____
_____
_____
_____

Comments

INGREDIENTS LIST

This is a list of all of the basic ingredients used in this book. Just add fresh fruits and vegetables:

IN THE FREEZER - MADE PREVIOUSLY
Good Stuff, Lasagna, Marinara Sauce, Milk Gravy, Okara Cubes, Okara Patties, Pesto, Polenta, Cooked Rice, Scrapple, Soy Milk Cubes, Soy Whiz, Tofu, Baked, Plain Tofu, Marinated Tofu

IN THE CUPBOARD - BAKING
Baking Powder, Baking Soda, Cornmeal, Cornstarch, Flour, Potato, Flour, Rice Flour, Unbleached, Whole Wheat, Dry Yeast

MILK
Rice Milk, Soy Milk

MISCELLANEOUS
Vegetarian Gelatin, Lemon Juice, Greek Olives, Potato Flakes, Raisins, Tomatoes - Canned, Sun Dried, Vegetable Juice, Wine

NUTS SEEDS AND OILS
Almonds, Cashews, Extra Virgin Olive Oil, Sesame Oil, Sunflower Seeds, Vegetable Oils, Walnuts

PASTA AND RICE
Spaghetti, Lasagna Noodles, Ramen, Rice-Brown, Balsamic and Wild

SEASONINGS AND FLAVORINGS
Almond Extract, Anise Seed, Basil - Fresh and Dried, Chili Powder, Cinnamon, Cloves, Coriander, Cumin, Fennel, Garlic, - Fresh, Minced and Powered, Ginger - Fresh and Powdered, Kitchen Bouquet, Lemon Pepper, Liquid Hickory Smoke, Marjoram, Mustard - Dry, Prepared and Dijon, Onions - Fresh, Dried and Powdered, Oregano, Parsley - Fresh and Dried, Pepper - Black, Red, Poultry Seasoning, Pumpkin Pie Spice, Sage, Salt, Savory, Thyme, Vanilla Powder, Vegetable Bouillon, Vegetable Broth, Vinegar -Balsamic, Rice and Apple Cider

SWEETENERS
Apple Juice Concentrate, Fructose, Honey, Molasses, Sugar

SAUCES
Soy, Teriyaki, Barbecue, Tomato, Worcestershire

INDEX

Ordering Information

Additional copies of The Soybean Family Tree are $12.95 each (plus sales tax of 7.25 % for Californians). Add $2.00 for shipping and handling. Mail checks or money orders to:

Bobbi Parker
Just Be Publications
5785 Fickett Lane Dept B
Paradise, CA 95969
(530) 877-3570

Write or call for quantity or wholesale prices.